CHIP CARVING

TECHNIQUES FOR CARVING BEAUTIFUL PATTERNS BY HAND

DANIEL CLAY

Foreword by **NANCY HILLER**

BLUE HILLS PRESS

"It is noticeable in countries quite remote from each other, how universal the chip-carving has been. The reason is not far to seek. Given a piece of wood and a knife, man would intuitively incise chequers, zigzags, circles, etc., upon the wood; and then, in order to obtain a richer effect, notch out the spaces between."

ELEANOR ROWE
Chip-Carving and Other Surface Carving, 1908

DEDICATION:
To Linda, Lauren, and Jean,
for lifelong support and inspiration.

Publisher & Editor: Matthew Teague
Design: Lindsay Hess
Assistant Publisher: Josh Nava
Layout: Alicia Freile
Photography: Daniel Clay
Index: Jay Kreider

Blue Hills Press
P.O. Box 239
Whites Creek, TN 37189

paperback: 978-1-951217-40-2
eBook ISBN: 978-1-951217-38-9
Library of Congress Control Number: 2022937859
Printed in the United States
10 9 8 7 6 5 4 3 2 1

Note: The following list contains names used in *Chip Carving* that may be registered with the United States Copyright Office: Klötzli; Pfiel.

The information in this book is given in good faith; however, no warranty is given, nor are results guaranteed. Woodworking is inherently dangerous. Your safety is your responsibility. Neither Blue Hills Press nor the author assume any responsibility for any injuries or accidents.

To learn more about Blue Hills Press books, or to find a retailer near you, email info@bluehillspress.com or visit us at www.bluehillspress.com.

CONTENTS

FOREWORD

When Daniel Clay asked me to consider writing a foreword for this book, my first response was "Why me?" I know nothing about chip carving, though I appreciate the skill this art form requires, and even more, the crisp, lively patterns it can produce. For several years I had admired Daniel's work, in addition to that of other chip carvers, but I had not so much as given chip carving a try. He replied that he and his publisher agreed I might offer a big-picture perspective on this specialized corner of our shared vocation as woodworkers.

That I can get behind. Woodworking has been my primary work and the foundation of my livelihood since 1980. While building furniture and cabinetry has been a largely solitary pursuit, I have long fed my interest in cultural history by reading, in addition to visiting museums. Over the past half-century I have seen significant cultural shifts, beginning with the 1960s rejection of consumerism and the delegation to others of practically all production from growing food to making clothing, or building and furnishing our homes. The young people my parents invited to move in with my family in the late '60s had an easy time convincing us that this divorce from most kinds of making had robbed our lives of worthy satisfactions, along with plain old valuable skills such as how to bake bread or build bookshelves.

Since the mid-2000s, there has been a blossoming of interest among young people in diverse specialized corners of woodworking, energized by the availability of instruction through internet platforms such as YouTube and Instagram, which enable enthusiasts to share images of their work and interact with each other. I know from experience that these interactions often grow from virtual engagement into what we have come to call real life. The conversations and new perspectives that arise from this engagement are changing our economies—from encouraging the formation of CSAs and farmers' markets to increasing opportunities for professional teaching at craft schools or via paid platforms online.

For me, one of the most exciting developments has been the creative application of long-established techniques to new expression. While many woodworkers have taken the capital-D design route of studio furniture making, which values individualism and innovation, others have looked backward as well as forward, embracing traditional techniques and adapting them in new forms.

My first encounter with this phenomenon (at least, the first such encounter that I can recall) was an exhibit of rustic furniture at the Adirondack Museum in Upstate New York around 2002. I had seen the occasional piece of furniture made with bent saplings and branches, but the gallery full of desks, tables, chairs, small boxes, and even wastebaskets making ingenious structural and decorative use of features of the living tree, especially in the case of birch bark, blew my mind. Fast-forward to the happy rediscovery that a naturally bent limb can make the ideal armbow for a stick chair. Several years ago Christopher Schwarz treated handsome pieces of boarded furniture as an art form by focusing on basic techniques and simple materials—not just as a means to achieve functional furnishings, but as worthy of respect in their own right. Schwarz's approach celebrated hand-milled boards and traditional, hand-driven nails at a time when most people were buying lumber pre-milled and shrink-wrapped at big-box stores, then assembling their work with pneumatic tools or drywall screws. Schwarz did the same with staked furniture.

Some dismiss the revival of simple, age-old forms as lacking in originality (as though true originality were not exceedingly rare). But pay attention to those materials – their grain and proportions; pay attention to the beauty and utility that result from even the simplest technique when you pursue it with meticulous care—and you end up with something elevated.

A similar focus on materials and methods has resulted in new takes on the traditional wooden spoon—spoons carved pristine, without adornment, some allowing their fluid forms to celebrate their origin in the branch of a tree, and others with crisp transitions from handle to bowl, some of them surface-carved or kolrosed by way of decoration. Hand-carved bowls by Danielle Rose Byrd and David Fisher offer other examples, as do bowls turned on a medieval pole lathe, a practice revived by British craftsman Robin Wood; 17th-century-style furniture made entirely by hand, from log to finished piece, by Peter Follansbee; the revival of seat weaving with natural rush and cattails gathered from a neighborhood marsh; or traditionally timber-framed buildings.

All of these examples focus unabashedly on traditional folk forms rather than privileging the individual artisan's aesthetic or aiming to be the most refined. While many artisans develop a recognizable personal aesthetic and turn these longstanding methods of making things into

their own art forms, whether with surface embellishment or by incorporating new motifs that challenge the white male domination of our craft, one element that differentiates these woodworkers from those of the capital-D school of design is that they fully embrace their role as carriers-on of tradition.

Daniel Clay is one of them, and a master of his art. Chip carving may be limited to the surface of things—a means of decoration, and so, perhaps easily dismissed by some. But as with any skill, mastering it takes discipline and practice. Don't take for granted those clean cuts, smooth lines, regular patterns, angles, and depths of cut, or the care required to achieve a precise and pleasing layout. They represent a pinnacle of craft. Fortunately, this book gives clear, step-by-step instructions on these and other dimensions of the chip carver's art.

One of the most attractive features of chip carving is its accessibility. You need only some flat boards, a means of holding them in place, and a few carving knives. Once you've mastered the basic techniques, you'll be ready to go beyond flat practice boards to transform pieces of furniture and other items. While chip carving in its most basic forms has been around for thousands of years, we have only seen the tip of the iceberg in terms of its potential applications. I for one am eager to see how others will apply it.

—Nancy Hiller

INTRODUCTION

The purpose of this book is to equip you with everything you need to know to become a skilled chip carver. If, like me, your reaction the first time you ever laid eyes on a skillful piece of chip carving was amazement bordering on disbelief that it could be done by human hands using a simple little knife, then you may be skeptical of the claim that the skills required to do it well could be communicated through a relatively short how-to book, and wholly incredulous if I told you that you can achieve significant success in chip carving in a matter of hours.

My own exploration of chip carving began with a how-to book and some carving knives I gave someone else as a Christmas present one year while living on the coast of Maine. The gifts sat untouched for a month or so before curiosity set in, amplified by mid-winter cabin fever, and I decided to give it a try myself. This is where, as a writer, I should probably avoid using the cliché "I was immediately hooked." But in truth I was. It grabbed me right away, and I think part of why it did was the shock of realizing that something that at first appeared so complex, so eye-popping, and presumably so difficult was actually . . . *not impossible*.

I imagine you have probably had a similar experience being captured by some new activity—the realization that here is something just accessible enough that you're not instantly discouraged, but not *so easy* that it fails to challenge and beguile you. It leads you to keep trying, and occasionally there are these little moments of effortless success, or at least hints at the possibility of success. They may be infrequent at first, and maybe then only the result of happy accidents, but they are enough to keep you at it.

As those little successes become more frequent and more intentional, a feeling grows inside of you. I bet you know the one I'm talking about. It is often expressed in phrases like, "Oh hey, look. I did it!" Or, "Oh yeah, I could really get into this." For someone new to chip carving it's usually something like, "Wow—when one of those little chips pops out it is *extremely satisfying*." I don't know if there is a single word for that feeling, but we could say it is the feeling of realizing "I can do this."

If you put the instruction in this book into practice, even if you have no prior experience with tools or woodworking, I predict you will have your own "I can do this" moment. I feel safe making that prediction for two reasons. First, I have seen that feeling bloom in beginning carvers over and over again in person while teaching classes and workshops around the country to a widely diverse body of students, many of whom have never touched a tool before. I've worked hard to make this book a distillation of how and what I teach in person. In it you will find advice on what tools and materials you need to get started, instruction on proper, safe carving technique, skill-building exercises, and carving projects ranging from simple and easy, to complex and challenging. My goal was to make the book the next best thing to learning in person, and if I have achieved that goal even to a small degree I see no reason not to expect similar results for you at home as I would if you attended one of my classes.

The second reason I have to expect success for you is more subtle, but I think it is very compelling. It is that chip carving is very, very old. Vastly older than how-to books and steel tools. If the relevance of that isn't immediately obvious, stay with me for a bit. To put it another way, we could say that chip carving is one form of something that is so old and universal that it contributes to the definition of what it means to be human: Humans make marks, and chip carving is a form of mark-making. Even if you don't know much about the details of how it works yet, in one sense, you were born for this.

I sometimes tell students in my workshops, "I know this seems a little tricky at first—and it does take some practice—but think about it this way: Have you ever carved your name or initials into something? Maybe a tree, or a school desk? Did anyone teach you how to do that? Probably not, right? Well, congratulations: You invented chip carving." The crux of that peculiar affirmation is that the raw mark-making impulse already belongs to you, and in the pages of this book you will find the guidance you need to develop, refine, and put it to creative use.

If we pressed a magic button that erased all knowledge of chip carving from existence, it would not be long before someone, somewhere—with only a sharp tool, a carvable surface, and the simple desire to convey some meaning, depict some aspect of nature or life, or mark an item as special or personal—would reinvent something very much like chip carving in a matter of minutes. Take a moment to imagine yourself as this person or their ancient counterpart. At first you make a scratch. You deepen that scratch to make it bolder and now the scratch is an incision. A second incision is made near the first to accentuate it even further and a chip pops out of the surface. You see that the mark you've made in the surface creates a play of light and shadow, and you like it, so you make another, and another, and so on.

This picture I've painted of someone naively following the ancient mark-making impulse in a world where chip carving doesn't yet exist as such, reminds me of another familiar scene: me, or maybe you, with a book at hand, carving one little chip at a time with a simple knife, gradually succeeding more and more at doing it well, spurred on by the satisfaction of those little moments of success. Before you know it, you're hooked.

—Daniel Clay,
Knoxville, Tennessee
May 6, 2022

1 GETTING STARTED— TOOLS & MATERIALS

This chapter contains all the information you need to get started chip carving—what to look for in a chip carving knife, sharpening gear and technique, what kinds of wood are suitable for chip carving, useful tools and techniques for laying out and transferring carving patterns, and suggestions for finding a good chip carving workspace.

One of the most attractive aspects of chip carving is the relatively low cost of entry. Unlike other types of woodworking (think furniture making, cabinetry, wood turning, etc.) you don't need to purchase or gain access to thousands of dollars of expensive gear, a dedicated workshop or a specialized workbench. In fact, you don't even need to buy a fancy chip carving knife. The knives I use throughout the book—and in nearly all of my carving otherwise—cost about $25 and they are widely available. They are not fancy or even particularly attractive, but they are perfectly adequate for doing high-quality work.

The same accessibility and friendly price-point holds true for chip carving materials as well. Most of the projects in this book are carved in basswood, which is inexpensive as far as hardwood lumber goes, and widely available, either through craft supply retailers or through your local lumberyard. For $30-40 you can buy enough basswood to keep you carving for weeks and weeks.

Availability and low cost notwithstanding, there are a few details you should be aware of before assembling your chip carving tool kit and material supply.

You don't need a shop or special workbench for chip carving. Any desk or table of medium to low height will do.

Low cost of entry: All you need to get started chip carving is a knife, a way to sharpen it, and a few pieces of basswood. I also suggest a non-skid rubber mat to go between the workpiece and the table—it helps keep things steady.

CHOOSING A CHIP CARVING KNIFE

Two knives from prominent knife manufacturers Klötzli and Pfiel. Both knives are made in Switzerland and designed to be used in the Swiss chip carving method. Note that Pfeil knives are a little larger than Klötzli knives.

The the Swiss-style chip carving knife has a perfectly straight edge, and the back of the blade curves to meet the angled blade at a sharp point.

The Klötzli knives (above, left) are slightly more refined than the Pfeil, but both are capable of great work in a wide variety of woods.

The "Swiss method" of chip carving gets its name, in part, from the fact that the primary tool it employs was given its contemporary form by Swiss carver Christian Rubi and Swiss knife maker Ernst Klötzli. Rubi and Klötzli developed their knife design for mass production in the 1950's, but evidence of tools with a similar shape predates their knife by at least 50 years. The design is now nearly synonymous with chip carving (largely thanks to carver and author Wayne Barton) and many versions are mass produced by large tool companies or in small batches by independent knife-makers around the world.

The knife's straight edge and sharp point are ideal for carving flat facets that intersect neatly at their edges to create crisp, clean chip pockets. The broad, arch-back profile provides strength to the thin blade, while the thinness, in turn, reduces the knife's tendency to wedge wood-fibers apart before the edge has a chance to cut them. The mirror (or near-mirror) polish of the sides helps the knife glide through the wood as the edge cuts. The angle of the blade in relation to the handle provides mechanical and ergonomic advantage, allowing the carver to make deep, powerful cuts with a minimum of effort or awkward body mechanics.

HOW TO SHARPEN A CHIP CARVING KNIFE

Perhaps the single most important sub-discipline in all of woodworking is learning how to sharpen the tools. Without sharp tools, you will not be able to do your best work. Period. A dull chip carving knife makes for laborious, tiresome carving and produces inconsistent, rough, or battered-looking carvings. Carving with a dull knife can be a very a discouraging experience. Conversely, as the old saying goes, "Sharp fixes everything." This may not be 100% true, but sharp certainly helps a lot.

I receive frequent requests from carvers for advice on how to improve their carving. They send me photos of their work and ask what they can do to make it cleaner or more precise. I can usually tell at a glance what the problem is, and nine times out of ten the culprit is a poorly sharpened knife, or bad blade geometry. Even flawless technique cannot entirely make up for a poorly tuned tool. As I said before, the Swiss method of chip carving is integrally tied to the specific design characteristics of the Swiss-style chip carving knife, and so for the techniques that comprise the method to work, the knife must be tuned-up in just the right way. It is not enough put a good sharp edge on the knife; the geometry of the entire blade must

Sharpening is a skill that takes practice. Be patient and follow the process described in the following pages carefully. The good news is that once your knife is sharp, keeping it sharp is relatively easy.

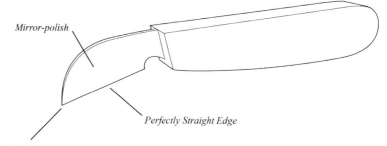

Mirror-polish

Perfectly Straight Edge

Needle-sharp Point

When sharpening, keep the point of the knife needle-sharp and the edge straight. Both sides should have a mirror or near-mirror polish, and the bevel should be rounded, not hard.

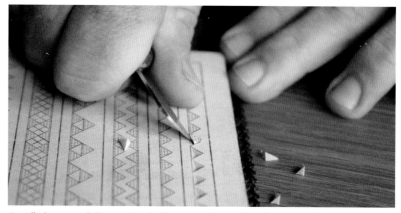

A well-sharpened chip carving knife can easily cut directly across the grain.

Resurfacing and reshaping a factory-fresh knife are two of the most important steps in sharpening a new knife: the factory-machined blade sides must be re-ground and a polished, and the hard-angled bevel must be rounded over.

The difference between a sharpened knife (left) and a knife directly from the factory is easy to see: the mirrored surface versus machine marks, a rounded bevel versus a hard machined bevel.

Sharpen on a whetstone by abrading the knife back and forth on the stone. To keep the edge of the straight hold the blade perpendicular to the direction of the stroke. As you work, use gentle downward pressure evenly along the length of the blade.

be right in order for it to do what it is supposed to.

Regardless of the claims made by manufacturers, mass produced edge-tools, such as knives, chisels, hand plane blades, etc., are never truly sharp or ready to use out of the box (though you may be able to open your mail with them in a pinch.) This holds true for mass produced chip carving knives as well, so before you begin carving with a brand new chip carving knife, you will need to tune it up.

SHARPENING GEAR

In the simplest terms, sharpening is the process of removing metal from both sides of a blade until they meet perfectly to form an edge. Metal is removed by rubbing the tool against an abrasive surface in a controlled manner and the most common tools for doing this are sharpening stones, or abrasive film applied to a very flat substrate, such as tempered glass, polished marble, melamine, or solid surface countertop material. The abrasive (the stones and the film do the same thing) removes small particles of metal and leaves behind tiny scratches on the knife. As you progress from a coarse to finer grits, the scratches left behind on the knife get smaller and smaller until you are left with a shiny mirror-like polish.

HOW TO SHARPEN A CHIP CARVING KNIFE (CONTINUED)

Choosing a sharpening system can be bewildering because of the sheer number of options and products on the market. The best advice I've ever heard on the subject is to simply pick one system and stick with it for a while. This is especially true when you're just learning to sharpen.

I use a combination of diamond sharpening stones and peel-and-stick abrasive film to tune up a new knife, however the entire process can be executed with abrasive film alone. This is the system I typically recommend for beginner carvers or anyone on a budget. The abrasive film can be obtained from any number of woodworking or auto-body suppliers and suitable flat substrate material can easily be found easily in most home improvement stores. You can also check flooring or countertop supply retailers—they can be great sources of scraps of flat-milled substrate materials that work great for sharpening.

Choose from a variety of sharpening stones: Solid diamond surface stones, a perforated diamond stone, and hard flat substrate with peel-and-stick abrasive film.

Peel and stick film can be cut into strips and applied to a substrate such as a polished marble tile or tempered glass.

Use scissors to trim abrasive film to size. I suggest an old pair because the abrasive will eventually dull the blades.

Carefully peel the backing off the film, not allowing anything to sick to it before adhering it to the substrate.

Adhere the abrasive to the substrate by starting at one end and smoothing it down with a finger to avoid air bubbles.

I use an array of six abrasive grits when tuning up and sharpening a new knife, as well as a leather strop charged with strop compound. Strop compound is simply a micro-abrasive particles suspended in a soft synthetic clay. The compound is rubbed onto a firm but flexible substrate, such as fine-grained leather glued to a wooden backing block. The knife is then pulled across the strop, and the micro-abrasive particles spread across the charged leather remove microscopic particles of leather. You'll know your strop is working if it turns black in the process of stropping.

The grits that I use to tune up and sharpen a new knife and their equivalent grit in microns can be seen at left. That said, there is nothing magical about my sharpening kit: If you already have a sharpening routine that works for you, stick with it.

Sharpening stones arranged from coarse to polishing, top to bottom. My own kit includes, from top to bottom: DMT Black Extra-Coarse / 60 micron; DMT Blue Coarse / 45 micron; DMT DIA-Flat Fine / 25 micron; DMT DIA-Flat Extra Fine / 9 micron; 3M Abrasive; Film 5 micron; 3M Abrasive Film 1 micron; FlexCut Gold Stropping Compound ~.6 microns.

HOW TO SHARPEN A CHIP CARVING KNIFE (CONTINUED)

Here is a summary of the steps for sharpening the knife. I go through this entire process on both sides of the knife at one grit before moving onto the next, finer grit:

- Work the sides.
- Work the edge at the proper angle—obtain/polish off a wire burr.
- Round over the bevel formed by abrading the sides and the edge.

WORK THE SIDES

To begin removing machine marks from the sides of the knife, start with a heavy grit sharpening stone lubricated with water and lay the knife down flat on one side. Stroke it back and forth a number of times, pressing it flat with light finger pressure. I usually do this in repetitions of about ten strokes—and then flip the knife over and repeat on the other side. You will begin to see the machine marks replaced by scratches from the sharpening stone. Do this for both sides of the knife until all the factory machine marks or scratches from the previous grit are replaced by scratches from the current grit.

WORK THE EDGE AT THE PROPER ANGLE

Swiss Chip Carving knives should be sharpened at an angle of approximately 8-10°. To obtain

Start resurfacing the sides by stroking the knife back and forth on the coarse stone with the blade held flat against the abrasive surface.

Use the full length of the stone when sharpening, with even downward pressure, and keep the edge of the knife perpendicular to the direction of the stroke.

Check your progress occasionally. Keep abrading the sides of the knife until the factory machine marks are replaced with scratches from the coarse stone.

The initial bevel angle is around 8-10°. To approximate the angle, place the knife flat on the stone, lift the back of the blade and slide a dime under the back.

The burr formed when sharpening can be seen as a long thin line reflecting light along the edge of the blade.

You can (carefully!) feel the burr formed on the edge of the blade as you sharpen. Do not break off the burr! It will fall off as you work through finer grits.

the proper sharpening angle, place the knife flat on the sharpening stone and lift the back of the blade about the thickness of a dime.

With the knife held at this angle, stroke the edge back and forth along the abrasive surface, pressing down gently and evenly, keeping the edge of the blade perpendicular to the direction of your strokes. It is important to distribute downward pressure evenly along the entire length of the blade, so that the edge remains perfectly straight.

As you work the blade in this manner, the metal at the very edge will begin to feather out and roll up to form what is known as a "wire burr." *This burr is very important* —the formation of a burr means that the side of the knife has been abraded to the point where it meets the opposite side of the knife. Though you can often see the burr as a bright reflective line along the length of the knife's edge, you can also check it by running a finger or thumb backwards across the side of the knife. The skin of your fingers is extremely sensitive, and if a burr has formed you should be able to feel it pretty easily.

Resist the urge to break off the burr on the knife's edge. As you progress through finer and finer grits, it will fall off on it's own.

HOW TO SHARPEN A CHIP CARVING KNIFE (CONTINUED)

ROUND OVER THE BEVEL

Before moving on to the next grit, round over the bevel between the sides and edge of the knife. Start with the blade held flat on the sharpening surface and begin stroking back and forth, as you continue stroking, repeatedly rock the blade up to the 8-10° sharpening bevel and back down to flat. This step is a little tricky at first—a little like simultaneously patting your head and rubbing your stomach. The goal is to obtain a smooth transition between the sides of the knife and the sharpened edge.

Now repeat the entire process—Work the sides, Work the edge, Round the Bevel—at each successively finer grit until the sides are polished, the wire burr has formed and fallen off or disintegrated, and the sides transition smoothly down to the sharpened edge with a slight convexity.

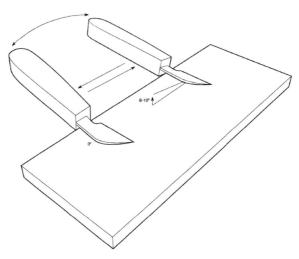

A two-part motion is used for rounding over the bevel; the knife is stroked back and forth against the stone while simultaneously being rocked up and down, from flat against the stone up to the 8-10° sharpening angle

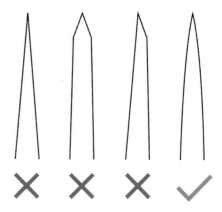

This illustration shows the cross-section geometry of a properly shaped knife blade: symmetrical, with a gradual, curved slope from the side to the sharpened edge.

The sharpening process is repeated through multiple grits until the burr has become detached from the edge of the knife and the entire blade is polished to a near-mirror finish.

A leather strop is simply a piece of leather glued to a flat block of hardwood and charged with a fine abrasive strop compound. Prepare the strop by rubbing its surface with the strop compound.

Strop the knife sides and the edge. Lay the knife flat against the compound-charged surface and pull backwards, applying light downward pressure.

At the end of the stropping stroke, lift the knife off the surface. Repeat this action several times for both sides of the knife.

The final surface of the knife should have a mirror or near-mirror like appearance.

STROPPING

The final step in sharpening is stropping the knife. Charge the strop with compound and pull the knife *backwards* across the charged strop surface. As the fine abrasive of the strop compound removes microscopic particles of metal the strop will turn black. Strop the sides and the cutting edge. Be careful at the end of each stroke not to flip the edge under and drag it across the strop surface as this will dull the edge.

WHEN TO SHARPEN & STROP

Once a brand new knife is tuned up—edge honed, sides polished, bevel rounded, and then stropped—you will probably not need to repeat the process in full very often unless the knife is damaged or dulled. It is a good idea however, to periodically re-hone the knife to touch up the sharpness of the cutting edge. To touch up the edge of your knife, resharpen the edge in the same manner described above starting with the second to last sharpening stone grit, followed by several strokes on the strop on each side of the blade. During carving it is a good idea to strop periodically as it keeps the knife's edge in top shape. Through practice you will get a feel for how often you need to strop or re-hone your knife.

SELECTING & PREPARING WOOD

Many types of wood can be chip carved, but the ideal wood for Swiss style chip carving, especially for the beginner, is basswood (*tillia*), also known in other parts of the world as linden or lime wood. Basswood is characterized by its tight straight grain, light creamy color, little to no figure (the patterned appearance of grain) and most importantly its softness, which allows it to be carved with a knife alone. Harder, denser woods such as oak or cherry may also be chip carved, but doing so often requires the use of mallet and chisel. Highly figured woods and exotic species with pronounced, spectacular grain patterns are not ideal because the appearance of the wood itself tends to compete and interfere with whatever is carved upon it. Basswood also has the advantage of being inexpensive and easy to come by.

There are many sellers that offer basswood blanks for carving in the form of flatsawn basswood boards and blocks, as well as items made of basswood such as small boxes, plates and platters.

The soft, even grain of basswood makes long, flowing, brush stroke-like cuts possible.

A second cut from the opposite direction frees the chip from the wood.

I prefer to buy large pieces of basswood lumber. Here I am "resawing" a two-inch thick board into thinner boards.

After resawing, the boards are taken to final thickness with a thickness planer.

Rough-cut basswood can be obtained at most commercial lumberyards or wood suppliers and milled into pieces suitable for carving projects.

Carvers with access to a woodworking shop may wish to purchase rough sawn basswood from a lumberyard and mill their own basswood lumber and make their own items. When picking out rough sawn basswood from the lumberyard, there are a few characteristics I look for in a board. It takes a little experience to spot the best boards at the lumberyard, especially when selecting from rough sawn stock. Here are the characteristics I look for when shopping for basswood at my local lumberyard:

- Straight boards with evenly colored grain and no knots
- Creamy white color
- I check the end grain to get an idea for how fast the tree grew—look for tight, narrow annual rings
- Lastly, if there are two boards of roughly the same size and apparent quality, I set them next to one another, pick them up one at a time and check their weight by feel. I'm afraid this isn't very scientific, but my rationale is that the heavier board likely has either a higher moisture content or is a little more dense, possibly due to slower growth. As both of these are desirable qualities, I typically choose the heavier of the two boards.

SELECTING & PREPARING WOOD (CONTINUED)

Other woods that may be chip carved with a knife include butternut, white pine, Spanish cedar, catalpa, and some species of mahogany. A number of softer hardwoods may be chip carved with a knife (walnut, for example) but may require working at a smaller scale. The best way to know if a wood can be chip carved is to give it a try. You'll quickly get a feel for how the wood responds, its limitations and characteristics.

After basswood, my favorite woods for chip carving in terms of ease of carving are butternut and white pine. Though I recommend you stick to basswood if you're just beginning to learn chip carving or dusting off neglected carving chops, once you gain a little bit of experience and confidence in your skills I suggest trying a project in one of those two woods. They each have their own "personality" as far as the carving experience goes, and if I can venture a prediction, I think you will find that switching to a wood with a slightly different character, especially one with which you're not familiar, will help you gauge just how important it is to pay attention to grain orientation, keep your knife sharp, and be attentive to the principles of good technique. This is a diplomatic way of saying that at first you may find switching woods challenging or

This Japanese-style toolbox is made of white pine, one of the easier woods to chip carve (next to basswood).

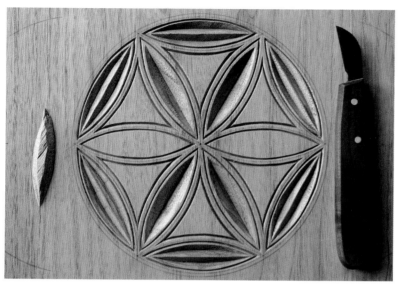

Butternut, sometimes called "white walnut," is another favorite for chip carving. I find butternut useful for designs on a slightly larger scale than basswood.

It is possible to chip carve black walnut, but it is not for the faint of heart; it's hardness makes for slow work.

Cherry can be chip carved, but not with the ease of softer woods like basswood, pine, and butternut.

Mahogany is yet another wood that can be chip carved, but doing so requires close attention to grain direction, sure-handedness, and quite a bit of sharpening.

even frustrating. I did. Stick with it, complete a project or two in a new species. In the end you will have a deeper understanding of the nuances of the carving process.

I am frequently asked, especially by furniture makers and other woodworkers, whether it is possible to chip carve hardwoods. The answer is a very qualified "yes." Hypothetically, any wood can be chip carved, but not every wood can be chip carved with the same tools and techniques. Obviously, you should not expect cherry or black walnut to respond the way basswood does. A chip pocket that may take three cuts to carve in softer woods is often more difficult to remove cleanly in a relatively dense hardwood like walnut, and designs composed of large chips may not be viable at all.

When it comes to denser, tough grained woods like oak and ash, you are unlikely to have much success with a knife. Some woods can only be carved with chisels struck by a mallet—these tools and techniques are beyond the scope of this book. The projects in this book are designed primarily for chip carving in basswood. It's the friendliest of chip carving woods, and I recommend you stick with it until you gain some experience and a firm grasp on basic chip carving techniques and concepts.

DRAWING & TRANSFERING PATTERNS

In this book I use two methods for applying carving patterns to the surface of workpieces: drawing directly on the wood in pencil and transferring patterns to the wood with a toner-print heat transfer.

TOOLS FOR DRAWING ON WOOD

Here are some useful tools for drawing patterns directly on the surface of the wood.

- Mechanical pencil, .5 mm lead, soft—I prefer a mechanical pencil because no sharpening is required and it produces lines of consistent width.
- Straight edge or ruler
- White Mars Rubber Eraser
- Pencil Compass—You could use a drafting compass with graphite drafting points. Sharpening graphite points requires more work, so I stick to a standard pencil compass.
- Combination square or speed square—A square aids in drawing straight lines that are parallel, perpendicular or 45° to the edges of a board.
- Dividers—Dividers are a kind of compass with two identical arms that terminate in sharp points. While sometimes used to scratch an arc or circle into a surface, they are also extremely useful for dividing a line into equal segments, or "stepping off" a series of equidistant points.

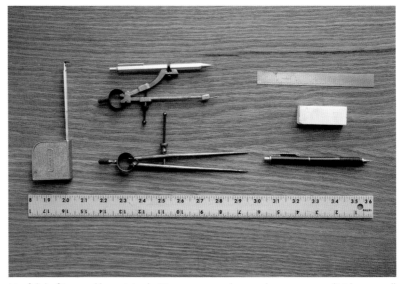

Useful drafting and layout tools: Tape measure, large ruler, compass, dividers, small ruler, white rubber eraser and mechanical pencil.

Dividers—one of the oldest tools for creating and understanding geometry—are used to measure, transfer and compare distances, and divide a given distance into equal increments.

Toner prints from a laser printer can be transferred to the surface of wood using heat. This only works with toner prints and will not work with inkjet prints.

Taping one edge of the print to the wood helps ensure that the print will not move during the transfer process.

Use overlapping strokes with the hot transfer tool, moving from the top taped edge of the print downward, working from the middle of the print out to either edge.

TONER PRINT HEAT TRANSFER

One of the most efficient ways of getting a carving pattern onto a wooden surface is using a pattern transfer iron and toner print. Laser printers and photocopiers make prints on paper by applying toner (instead of ink) to the paper with heat. The prints that these machines make can be transferred by placing them face down on the wooden surface and heating the back with strokes from a pattern transfer tool, a small heating iron with a circular brass heating element. Pattern transfer irons are widely available from craft and hobby suppliers.

First, be sure that your print was made by a laser printer or photocopy machine. Prints from inkjet printers are not transferable. Tape the pattern printed side down onto the surface. Blue painter's tape works very well for this.

Allow the iron to heat up, and make overlapping passes across the back of the toner print. The heat from the iron can cause the paper to buckle and stretch. To prevent this warping from creating a warped pattern, work from the center of the print out, using overlapping strokes that start close to the tape line and move away from it. Use your other hand to hold the bottom of the pattern flat against the wood.

SELECTING & PREPARING WOOD (CONTINUED)

The iron will melt some of the toner and the pattern should stick lightly to the surface. Start from the bottom of the taped pattern print, pull an inch or so of the pattern away from the wood, and check the quality of your transfer.

There will likely be spots you need to iron again. Proceed like this, spot ironing any trouble spots and gradually pulling more of the pattern away from the wood until the entire pattern is transferred.

WORKSPACE & WORK-HOLDING

Unlike other types of woodworking, no special workspaces or workbenches are needed for chip carving. Some carvers prefer to carve seated with the work held in their lap. Personally I prefer working on a low table or desk top near a window with good, indirect daylight. Because I am right handed, I orient myself with the window to my left so that the knife and my work are clearly illuminated, and the raking light produces good shadows in the chip pockets as I work. I avoid carving in spaces with evenly defused light that produces no shadows—shadows are what give a chip carving its character, so I like to see them as I progress through a piece. I also avoid carving under lights suspended directly above or behind

The heat from the transfer tool will cause the toner print to adhere to the surface of the wood—fight the temptation to peel back the entire print at once. Instead, peel back only an inch or two and check for spots that need to be touched up.

Continue to check for poorly transferred spots and reapply the iron as necessary, peeling back a little more of the pattern print each time.

Good light makes carving much easier and more pleasant. I prefer to sit near a window with diffuse or indirect daylight coming from the direction of my non-knife hand.

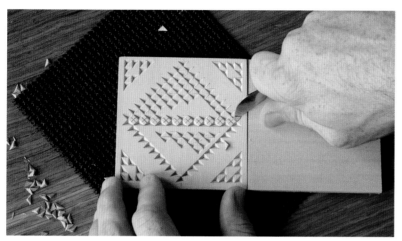

A piece of non-slip rubber mat beneath the workpiece prevents it from sliding around as you work.

me because the work gets lost in the shadows cast by my hands, head and body.

For the sake of safety, it is a good practice to place a piece of a rubber non-slip mat (made for putting under throw rugs) between the workpiece and the table top. This helps keep the work in place as you carve.

For some pieces, such as this 6" square butternut box, a table or desk top simply doesn't work very well as a workspace because the size of the piece effectively raises the surface of the work too high for comfortable safe carving. In these situations I opt to work either in my lap, holding the piece against my body for stability, or sometimes with the work held between my legs and resting on the chair.

Some pieces are easier to carve when held in your lap; If I tried carving this box on the table, the surface would be 6" higher than the table top, reducing my leverage and control of the knife.

2 | BASICS OF TECHNIQUE

Swiss-method chip carving is one of the safest, most accessible, and most versatile technical approaches to wooden surface carving. In this chapter you will learn the two standardized knife grips used in the Swiss method, the body mechanics that power them, and the basic process of carving simple chips.

KEY CONCEPTS

GRIPPING THE KNIFE

Swiss chip carving is done primarily with a single knife, using two knife grips that we will call First Position and Second Position.

The purpose of theses two distinct grips is to create opposing incisions that mirror one another at a consistent angle; the angle of cut in First Position should mirror the angle of cut in Second Position closely as possible. This means that all of the resulting chips will have a V-shaped cross-section.

MAINTAINING CONTACT

One of the defining characteristics of the Swiss method is that some part of the knife hand, either the thumb or the knuckles, maintains contact with the workpiece at all times. These points of contact provide stability and control, which in turn, makes the technique relatively safe.

The thumb or knuckles provide tactile feedback and the ability to "brake" should the knife slip out of the cut being made. "Planting" the thumb or knuckle of the knife hand on the workpiece also provides leverage—your thumb and knuckles become pivot points, or fulcrums allowing your shoulder and arm to act together as a power source and lever. This places a tremendous amount of cutting power at the tip of the knife, and gives you a high degree of control.

First Position knife grip.

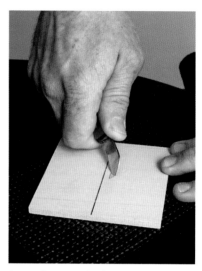
Second Position knife grip.

Keeping the thumb or knuckles in contact with the workpiece at all times provides stability, control, and leverage while you work.

Second Position angle of cut should match First Position angle of cut.

THREE CUTS, ONE CHIP

ESTABLISHING THE FIRST POSITION KNIFE GRIP

1

Cradle the knife along the inside of your first knuckle joint, blade point out, edge away from you.

2

Wrap your fingers around the handle.

3

Place your thumb against the side of the handle. Keep the knife and hand locked in this position to work as a unit.

4

The blade should be roughly parallel to your thumbnail.

The following three-cut sequence is the technical foundation of all Swiss-style chip carving in a tiny, triangular nutshell. Following this sequence carefully will teach you to:

- Establish proper First and Second Position knife grips and commit them to muscle memory
- Use both grips to create cuts with matching angles
- Use body mechanics to carve safely with maximum power and knife control

I strongly recommend you spend plenty of time practicing carving these little triangular chips, also known as three-cornered chips. For that reason, the first several rows of Practice Board 1 in the following chapter are made up almost entirely of three-cornered chips in various configurations and sizes.

ESTABLISH THE FIRST POSITION KNIFE GRIP

Hold your hand out, with the palm up. Place the knife across the inside of your first knuckle joint, with the blade out and up. Wrap your fingers around the handle and plant the inside of the first joint of your thumb on the handle near the base of the blade. Check your grip by looking down the blade—your thumbnail and the blade should be roughly parallel to one another. Lock your hand in this position.

THREE CUTS, ONE CHIP (CONTINUED)

CUT #1

Plant the tip of your thumb on the workpiece and position the tip of the knife at the top of the triangular chip, with the blade held about 55°-65° to the wood.

(An easy way to stay oriented properly to these little triangular chips is to think of them as pyramids. For this first cut we're starting with the tip of the knife at the top of the pyramid.)

To make the first cut, keep your wrist straight and raise your elbow slightly, using your planted thumb as a pivot point or fulcrum. At the same time, plunge the tip of knife to plunge into the wood. As the knife plunges into the cut, the edge of the blade should follow the line all the way to the base of the triangle.

ESTABLISH THE SECOND POSITION KNIFE GRIP

To establish a Second Position grip, start by holding the knife in a First Position grip, then simply rotate the knife in your hand until your thumb rests on the back of the knife, similar to how you might hold a box cutter or utility knife to open a package. Once again, lock your hand in this position.

MAKING CUT #1

First cut, First Position. Thumb on workpiece, tip of the blade at the top of the triangle.

Tip of the knife plunges into the wood at 55°-65° angle. Thumb maintains contact with the workpiece.

ESTABLISHING THE SECOND POSITION KNIFE GRIP

Rotate the knife, place thumb on the back of the blade. Keep the knife and hand locked with a gentle but firm grip.

The blade is roughly perpendicular to your thumbnail.

MAKING CUT #2

Second cut, Second Position. Knuckle on workpiece, tip of the blade at the top of the triangle.

Tip of the blade plunges into the wood at 55°-65° angle. Knuckle maintains contact with the workpiece.

CUT #2

Before we make the second cut, rotate the workpiece roughly 120° counterclockwise.

Now, with your hand locked in Second Position, plant your knuckle(s) on the workpiece and position the tip of the knife at the top of the triangular chip, (the top of the pyramid) the same point your first cut began, once again with the blade at about a 55° - 65° angle to the wood. This angle should mirror the angle of the first cut as closely as possible.

To make the second cut, once again, lift your elbow with your wrist held straight, and plunge the tip of the knife into the wood, with the edge of the knife following the line of the triangle all the way to the base line.

CUT #3

For the third and final cut, leave the workpiece positioned as it is and return to a First Position grip on the knife.

Plant the tip of your thumb on the workpiece and position the tip of the knife on the point of the triangular chip farthest away from you. This is the point where your first cut terminated. Once again, the knife should be held at that same 55 - 65° angle to the wood.

This final cut will relieve the chip from the board. This cut is a little different. Whereas the first two cuts were plunge cuts, this cut

THREE CUTS, ONE CHIP (CONTINUED)

is made with a drawing or pulling motion. To make this cut, as you lift your elbow and pivot on your thumb to lower the tip of the blade into the wood, simultaneously draw or pull the knife across the baseline of the triangle. This is done in a single motion, with your hand remaining locked in First Position.

If you've made all of your cuts properly the chip should pop free of the wood with a little click! sound, leaving a clean, faceted pocket where the chip once was.

If the chip does not release itself from the wood that means your cuts do not intersect and the chip is being held in place by un-severed wood fibers. Do not try to pry the chip out of the wood with your knife! Attempting to pry a stubborn chip from the wood risks bending or breaking the tip of the knife in the workpiece and will almost certainly result in an ugly, chewed up-looking chip pocket. Instead of digging or prying, simply repeat the entire sequence cuts from the beginning, using your existing cuts as guides, deepening each cut until all three cuts intersect and the chip pops free. You will find additional troubleshooting tips in the following chapter, Practice Boards.

MAKING CUT #3

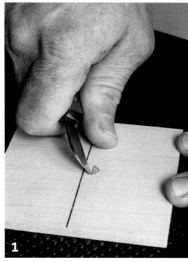

1 Third cut, return to First Position. Tip of the blade on far corner of triangle, thumb in contact with the workpiece.

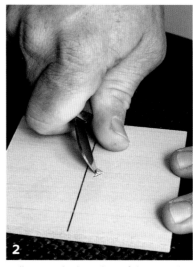

2 Pull across the base line of the triangle as you lower the knife into the wood. This cut is more of a slice than a plunge.

3 If all of the cuts intersect, the chip pops out cleanly.

CARVING LINES

Knife and hand locked in First Position, the thumb rides across the surface of the wood and the blade follows.

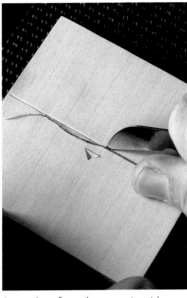

Second cut from the opposite side relieves the chip.

Long, straight or curved lines are typically carved by making two opposing cuts in First Position, with the knife hand riding on the thumb. You will be tempted to glue your eye to the blade, in the hope of preventing it from wandering from the line. Instead, try following the line itself with your eye, keeping your focus a little ahead of the knife's cutting edge, and letting the knife follow where your eye leads.

Make your first cut in First Position along one edge of the line. Now rotate the workpiece 180° and make an opposing First Position cut along the opposite side to relieve the long thin chip from the board.

Lines carved across the width of a board provide a glimpse of the V-shaped cross section common to all chips carved using the Swiss method.

Chip carved "lines" are actually V-groove chips. The wider the line, the deeper the groove.

3 | PRACTICE BOARDS

If you have not yet read and worked through chapter 2, The Basics Of Technique, it is crucial that you do so before proceeding. All the foundations of Swiss chip carving technique are contained in the sequence described in chapter 2. Everything in these practice boards (and the patterns in the rest of the book) assume that you have achieved some level of proficiency at carving these simple triangular chips.

PRACTICE BOARD 1

ROWS 1 - 4

Rows 1-4 will give you plenty of opportunity to hone the basic three-cut sequence. Here are some suggestions on how you should proceed.

Start in the middle of the row so that your thumb or knuckles have plenty of workpiece surface to make contact with. When you get close to an edge of the practice board, use a scrap or another board of the same thickness as a bracing surface for your thumb or knuckle.

Carve one chip at a time, working through the entire three-cut sequence for each chip until it has been removed from the board. Examine results and adjust accordingly on the next chip.

For example, if the center point of your chip pockets are off-center, it is because your First and Second Position cutting angles do not match. To fix the problem, increase or decrease the angle of cut for one (or both) positions. Take your time on these first few rows. Working out the kinks at this stage of learning will make all the other techniques, concepts and carving patterns in the book much more accessible.

First cut, First Position

Second cut, Second Position

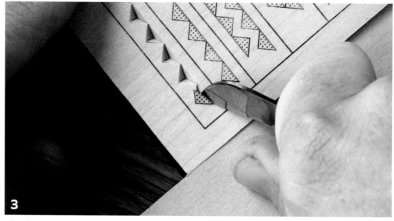

Third cut, First Position. If all of the fibers have been cleanly severed the chip will pop free.

1
Notch chips are removed with two cuts to define the stylized flower petals.

Press the knife toward the center of the flower in one position, then the other.

3
The v-shaped notches that define the petals intersect with the surrounding triangular chips that define the overall shape of the stylized flowers.

ROW 5

Row five is a simple example of compound chip shapes—two differently shaped chips intersect to give the appearance of a row of simple, stylized flowers.

The first step is to remove the shaded triangular chips. These chips are identical in size and shape to the chips in rows 1-4.

Next, remove the small notch chips. Removing these small notch-shaped chips will define the petals of each tiny flower.

These chips are removed by cutting across the wall of the already-removed triangular chips, toward the center of the flower.

You will make two cuts for each little notch—a First Position cut and Second Position cut. The cuts for carving the notch chips are not plunge cuts or pulling cuts, but what I call a press cut. Hang just a little bit of the tip of the knife over the edge of the diamond-shaped flower, with the blade aligned to one side of the notch. Now press the knife into the diamond, until the blade reaches the center of the flower. Be gentle—the diamond-shaped flowers are delicate, and you don't need to use much pressure for carving such tiny notches. Now switch positions and make another press cut on the other side of the notch.

PRACTICE BOARD 1 (CONTINUED)

ROW 6

Row 6 introduces adjacent chips, or chips that share a chip-pocket wall with one another. This is a very common design element in many chip carving patterns.

In this example, the shared wall crosses the grain. This presents a technical challenge that requires a change in the sequence of cuts made to remove the chips so they can be removed without damaging or removing the shared wood.

Remove the top triangular chip with the Three Step method, as before. The adjacent chip will be removed with the same three cuts, but in a different order.

First, using First Position, cut along the baseline of the adjacent chip, away from the first chip pocket. This is a good general rule of thumb: whenever possible, carve away from existing chip pockets. By making this cut first, you are severing the short grain fibers between the two chip pockets. Next, turn the practice board 120° clockwise and make a First Position cut on the right side of the chip. Finally, make a Second Position cut along the left side of the chip. This cut will relieve the chip from the board. After you have removed all the large chips that share a wall, move on to the tiny three-cornered chips between.

Cut away from the adjacent chip pocket first.

Next, make a First Position cut from the top of the triangle down to the base.

The final cut begins at the top of the triangle.

A slightly longer line requires a combination of plunge cut and pull cut.

All of the cuts are made using the First Position.

The relief cut is made across the grain.

If all of the cut angles match, the bottom point of the chip pocket will be centered.

ROW 7

The chips in row 7 are equilateral triangles, and have a larger surface area than the small right triangles that make up rows 1 - 6. This row will give you a feeling for carving slightly larger chips.

With this row you can also begin to experiment carving entirely in First Position, using drawing/pulling cuts as opposed to plunge cuts.

Alternately, you can mix and match First and Second Position cuts for these chips. If you take this approach, you will find that equilateral triangles are a good challenge because they leave you nowhere to hide: If your First and Second Position cutting angles do not mirror one another perfectly, it will be glaringly obvious.

If you try only one of these approaches, try carving exclusively in First Position. Using a single position makes it easier to achieve a consistent cutting angle. Later we explore mixing different cutting angles, but for now, focus on consistency. First Position also typically offers the greatest stability and maneuverability, making it useful for executing difficult applications like carving long flowing curves, so it's a good idea to become very comfortable with carving in First Position.

PRACTICE BOARD 1 (CONTINUED)

ROW 8

Row 8 is made up of elongated triangles of differing widths.

This row will give you some additional practice in making long, drawing cuts in First Position.

I recommend carving the long sides first for each triangle, followed by a relieving cut along the baseline.

Remember that the larger the surface area of a chip is, the deeper its chip pocket will be (assuming, of course, that all of the facets are carved at the same angle), and the deeper a chip pocket is, the darker a shadow it will create. The balance of shadow & light affects the overall visual impact of a carving, therefore, when a carving pattern employs both large and small chip shapes it's a good idea to slightly lower the angle used to carve the larger chip pockets.

Making this slight change will keep the larger chip pockets from being too deep, and help balance the intensity of their shadows with those of smaller chip pockets. Experiment with slightly decreasing the angle of cut as you proceed through the increasingly wider triangles. But don't overdo it! The change in cutting angle I'm describing is very slight.

Alter the depth of long pull cuts as necessary. From top to bottom, the cut goes from shallow to deep.

Cutting from the bottom to the top the cut plunges from deep to shallow

Make a relief cut along the baseline of the chip.

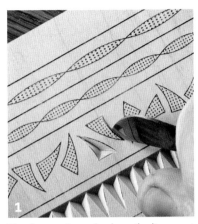

The first cut is made along the line most parallel to the grain.

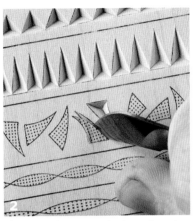

The second cut is made along the other long side.

The relief cut is made along the base line, across the grain.

ROW 9

Row 9 is made up of curved triangular chips set at different angles to the grain direction of the wood.

The purpose of this row is to further your awareness on the role that grain direction plays in sequencing your cuts in order to remove chips cleanly.

For this row it is recommended that you make all cuts in First Position. The order of the cuts—which lines you cut first—depends on the chip's orientation to the grain.

The rule of thumb to employ here is this: Whenever possible, cut the lines that run parallel to the grain first, followed by the next most parallel and so forth. Carving the lines that run parallel to the grain first reduces the possibility that the chip will split out along that line, like a tiny piece of firewood.

For most of these chips there is more than one order of cuts that will work well. Each different orientation appears twice, so you have two chances to try different ordering scenarios for each one.

PRACTICE BOARD 1 (CONTINUED)

ROW 10 & 11

Until now all the chips in the practice board have been triangular in shape—also known as three-cornered chips—and have required three cuts to be removed. The pointy, oblong chips—two-cornered chips—in these two rows will be removed by making two identical cuts in opposing directions.

For these chips you will make all of your cuts in First Position, pulling or drawing the knife through each cut. The cuts start shallow, deepen as you near the middle of each chip, and get shallower toward the end.

Always try to only cut as deeply as necessary to create a chip. Cutting too deep often results in undercutting and weakening wood that you may not want to remove.

When making curved cuts it is common for the knife to skip, or "chatter" through the cut, leaving a chip pocket wall, or facet, with a rough, or stepped surface. To prevent chatter, tip the butt of the knife up as you cut—this effectively reduces the width of the blade, from edge to back, that is being pulled through the curved cut. Try to make this adjustment without changing your angle of cut.

The cut begins shallow and increases in depth toward the middle.

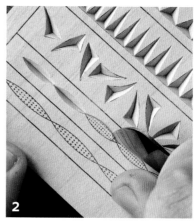

Decrease depth of cut as you approach the end of the line.

The relief cut is made in the same way.

PRACTICE BOARD 2

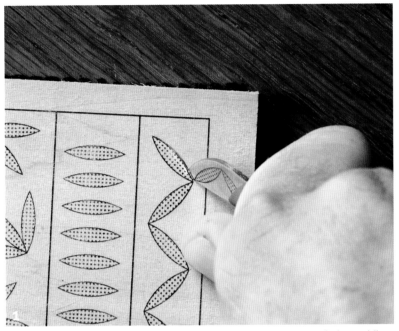

As before, begin with a shallow depth of cut, deepen as you approach the middle, and reduce depth of cut toward the end.

The relief cut is identical to the first cut. Try to keep your angle matched for a perfectly symmetrical chip pocket.

ROW 12

Row 12 consists of two-cornered chips set at an angle to the direction of the grain. This row will give you some additional practice carving two-cornered chips like the ones in rows 10 & 11, but there's also something else to learn here. Pay attention to the way it feels to make theses cuts at an angle to the grain as opposed to directly across it, like the two previous rows. Carving diagonally to the grain tends to feel a little smoother, and indeed, chips oriented diagonally to the grain are often easier to remove cleanly.

Remember to keep the knife tipped up a little on the blade axis when making curved cuts to help prevent the blade from skipping or chattering through the cut.

PRACTICE BOARD 2 (CONTINUED)

ROW 13

By now you should have developed some muscle memory for carving two-cornered chips. In this row we alter the technique slightly to facilitate cleanly carving two-cornered chips oriented parallel to the grain.

First, make a cut along one of the chips as you did for the other two-cornered chips, using First Position, with the knife tipped up slightly along its blade axis as you pull through the curved cut.

For the opposing cut—the relief cut—make an identical cut, but as you approach the middle of the line, lift your knife out of the wood just a little, finishing the line with a shallow cut that severs only the upper fibers of the chip.

Upon finishing your second cut, you will probably find that the chip is loose, but not yet free from the board. Don't try to pry it out! Instead, repeat your second cut, severing the wood fibers below the surface that are holding the chip in place.

You may find that you leave a tiny little piece of waste in the bottom of the chip pocket. Remove that waste by repeating cuts on one or both sides until you sever the wood fibers holding it in place.

The first cut is made with the same shallow-deep-shallow progression used on two-cornered chips in the previous two rows.

The relief cut starts the same as the first cut.

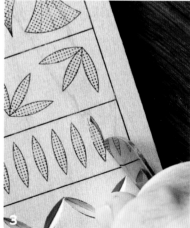

Reduce the depth of the relief cut early.

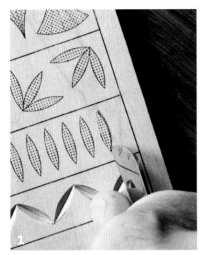

Finish the relief cut at a shallow depth.

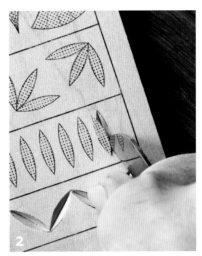

Repeat the cut to relieve the chip.

Why does this work? Your first cut severed one half of the fibers holding the chip in place. If you were to try to relieve the chip from the board by making an identical opposing cut at full depth, the chip would very likely want to split off from the board like a tiny piece of firewood, and the split could "run" into wood that you don't intend to remove. Lifting your knife halfway through the cut allows the bottom of the chip to stay anchored while the knife severs the upper fibers of the chip cleanly.

If this subtle but useful alteration to the process feels awkward at first, don't worry, you're not alone. It took me a little while to get the hang of it myself. It is a technique that is well worth spending some time on because it can greatly improve your ability to carve clean curves that turn back and forth across the grain. Like the other fine-motor skill operations that comprise good technique and knife-control, it will eventually become part of your muscle memory.

Controlling depth of cut is the key to cleanly removing two-cornered chips that follow the grain.

PRACTICE BOARD 2 (CONTINUED)

ROW 14

To carve the configurations of two-cornered chips in this row cleanly you'll use the technical concepts introduced in the last few rows—tipping the knife up on it's blade-edge axis for curved cuts, and strategically controlling the depth of cut when relieving a two-cornered chip that runs parallel to the grain—as well a new, crucially important technique: rolling the knife into and out of your primary cutting angle to prevent undercutting wood between adjacent chip pockets.

Each motif in this row contains three two-cornered chips converging to a common point. In order to preserve the wood that separates the chips near their shared points, it is crucial that you do not aggressively undercut the wood that separates them. This should be achieved primarily by controlling your depth of cut, but you can further ensure that the tip of the knife does not cut too deeply under wood you want to preserve by increasing the cutting angle at the beginning and/or end of the cut. In other words, you must change your cutting angle as you cut, i.e. roll the knife through the cut.

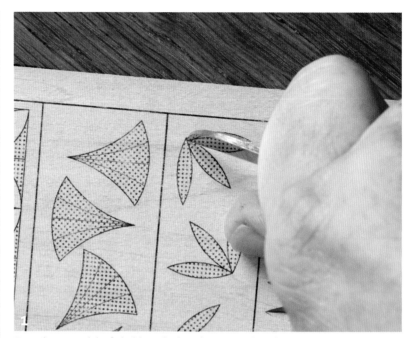

Start the cut with knife held at a higher-than-normal angle so as not to undercut the wood between chips.

As you cut, "roll" the knife down into the primary angle of cut.

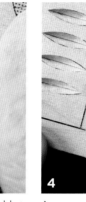

3 Start the relief cut with the knife held at the primary cutting angle.

4 As you near end of the cut, roll the knife into a higher angle of cut.

5 For this cut, there's no need to change angles as you cut; use the primary angle of cut along the entire length.

6 For the final cut, start with the primary angle of cut and roll the knife up as you approach the point where the chips converge.

Starting with the first motif in the row, make your first cut on the right side of the vertical chip.

Relieve that chip by rotating the board 180°, and beginning your cut at the point where your last cut terminated. As you begin this relief cut notice that the tip of your knife is pointed toward the adjacent chips and the wood that separates them. To avoid undercutting, begin the cut with your knife at a steeper angle than usual, about 85-90° to the surface of the wood, and as you proceed through the cut lower or roll the knife down to your primary cutting angle of about 55°-65° degrees. Proceed through the relief cut, adjusting your depth of cut as necessary to prevent the chip from splitting away from the board.

Repeat for the second and third chips in this motif, remembering to roll the knife out of or into a steeper angle of cut near the point where the chips converge.

PRACTICE BOARD 2 (CONTINUED)

ROW 15

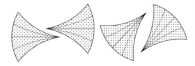

Fan motifs are among the most iconic design elements in the design vocabulary of chip carving, and once again, carving them cleanly requires you to utilize all the technical concepts you've learned so far: combining depth, angle and order of cut to cleanly remove only the chip and not the wood around it.

Begin with the first long, curved triangle of the first fan motif. Your first cut will be made from the wide part of the triangle down to the point where all the fan chips converge.

Rotate the board 180° for the opposing cut. Begin this cut at a higher angle than your primary cutting angle, and with a very shallow depth of cut.

As you draw the knife through this cut and lower the tip of the knife deeper into the wood, roll the cutting angle down to your primary cutting angle.

The third cut is made across the grain, along the short side of the triangle, to relieve it from the board.

Proceed through the fan chips one at a time across the board.

The first line of each chip should be carved away from previously carved chips. For example,

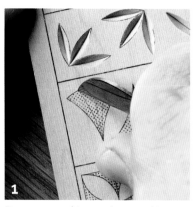

1. Remove one chip at a time, working across the fan motif.

2. First cut is made away from the center of the fan.

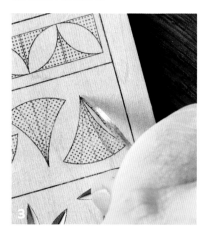

3. Start at the tip of the fan, with a high cutting angle.

4. Roll the knife down into the primary cutting angle.

Make the relief cut across the grain.

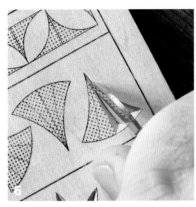

Use a higher angle of cut at the point end of the fan chips.

Roll into the primary angle of cut as you approach the wide end of fan chips.

Reverse the process when starting at the wide end of a fan chip. Start the cut using the primary angle of cut.

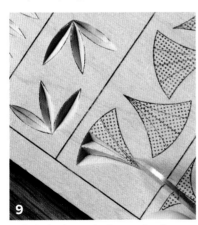

Roll the knife to a higher angle of cut as you approach the narrow end.

The relief cut is made across the grain.

to carve the second chip in the first fan motif, you'll need to carve away from the chip you've already removed. That means you'll need to begin with the board upside down, starting your first cut at the point of the fan, with your knife held at a higher angle, rolling the knife down into your primary cutting angle as you draw the knife through the cut.

Take a look at this drawing of the fan motif and notice that chips do not actually converge to a shared point. The two inner chips of the fan are staggered in length, and both are slightly shorter than the outside chips. This is how you should try to carve your fan motifs, and here's why: There simply isn't enough space at the tip of the fan for all four chips to converge. Stopping the inner two chips a little short of the tip of the fan allows all four chips to be carved cleanly, and still give the appearance of a fan motif with a neat, sharp point."

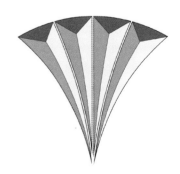

PRACTICE BOARD 2 (CONTINUED)

ROWS 16 & 17

The border patterns in rows 16 & 17 contain pairs of chips that share a chip pocket wall and converge to a shared point, similar to the chips in the fan motif. This means that you will need to control your depth and angle of cut precisely (as you did when carving the chips of the fan motifs) to avoid excessive undercutting that might weaken the shared chip pocket wall.

Make the first cut for each chip with the grain, along the line that represents the center ridge of the wall that is shared with the adjacent chip pocket. The second cut is made along the curved side of the three-cornered chip. Finally, relieve the chip by carving across the grain along the baseline of the chip.

The triangular chips in row 17 are removed with the same order of cuts used for the chips in rows 1-3.

The first cut is made with the grain.

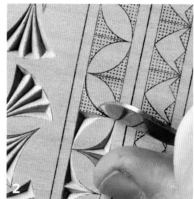

The second cut is made along the curvy side of the chip.

The relief cut is made across the grain.

Triangular chips are removed last, using the same order of cut as the chips in the first four rows of Practice Board 1.

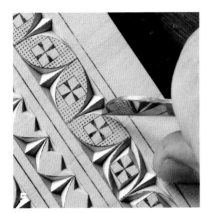

Make the first cut across the grain.

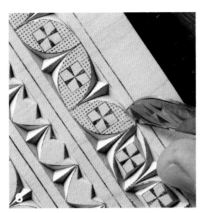

The cut begins shallow and is deepest at the end.

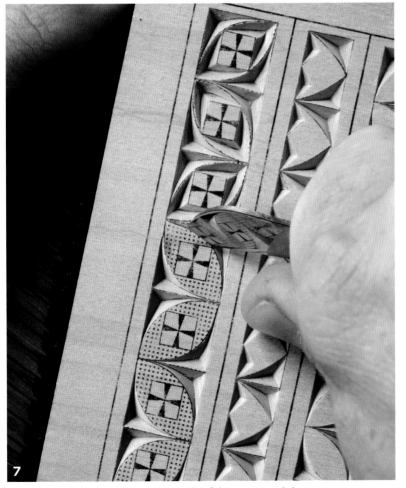

The second cut is made on the other side of the compound chip.

ROW 18

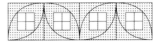

The border pattern in row 18 is typically referred to as a "Gothic border." Note its similarity to the pattern in row 16, and the central stylized flower motif similar to the pattern in row 5. There's a reason that this pattern is the final row of the practice boards: it requires you to put all of the technical concepts and skills you have learned in previous rows to work. In order to carve it cleanly you must be attentive to your depth and angle of cut, follow a specific order of operations and keep grain direction in mind.

The first phase of carving the Gothic border pattern is to remove the pairs of adjacent chips that define the petal shapes. Follow the same order of operations described for the pattern in row 16.

Next, remove the birdsmouth shaped chips that define the flower in the center of each petal. These are compound chips so they are removed in stages. First, cut along the curved sides of the petal. To reduce the risk of splitting, make the first cut on the curved line that crosses the grain.

PRACTICE BOARD 2 (CONTINUED)

ROW 18 (CONTINUED)

The cut to relieve the first of the two chips that form the compound birdsmouth shape is made across the grain alongside the central flower shape. This cut is not drawn on the practice board, you will have to eyeball where this cut begins or ends. It extends directly across the birdsmouth shape like this:

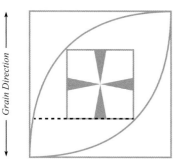

The final relief cut should be obvious—it is made with the grain alongside the adjacent edge of the central flower. After the chips around the flower are carved, carve the notches that define the petals, using the process described on page 41.

Now, a confession: This border pattern gave me fits when I first attempted it. I simply could not make it all come out cleanly. It takes a fair amount of knife control and attentiveness to grain, and a very sharp knife—skills that take practice to develop. If you have trouble, do your best and move on, but do try again at a later date.

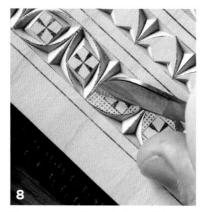

8 Carving across the grain first will help prevent splitting.

9 Carve all the way across the compound chip.

10 The last piece of the compound chip is made with the grain.

11 The cut ends with the tip of the knife down in the center of the chip pocket.

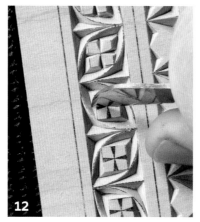

12 Lastly, remove the notch chips to define the flowers.

13 Use alternating First and Second Position cuts as in Row 5.

BORDER LINES

Line cuts are made in First Position, thumb riding on the workpiece.

Train your eye on the line, a little bit ahead of the blade.

The thumb rides against the wood for the entire length of the cut. Take the cut all the way to the corner.

There's one more lesson to be learned from the practice board: carving the border lines.

The long cuts necessary to carve the border lines may seem intimidating at first, but it is easier than it looks. It's best to dive in and not worry too much about precision at first. Much more important than precision is internalizing the feeling of the motion of the cut.

Long cuts tend to turn out smoother when done in a single fluid pass, with your hand on "auto-pilot" following where your eye leads it, rather than with a halting, too-slow or over-cautious attitude, worrying about every little wiggle or tendency of the knife to stray off the printed pattern.

Think about it like this: If you were to make a long cut in First Position, drawing the knife through the wood in a long straight or curved line, not to a printed or drawn pattern, but just improvising, the resulting line would likely be relatively smooth and fair. Why? Because you're not focused on following a pattern. The mark you make is coming from the motion of your body, and it's easy to pull your hand across the wood in a fairly smooth motion.

The difficulty comes in steering the cut to follow the pattern; it requires the coordination of your eye and your body.

BORDER LINES (CONTINUED)

One technique is to train your eye to look just ahead of the knife, instead of directly at the tip of the knife. This is similar to the way you drive a car, not looking directly at the part of the road that is just a few feet in front of your wheels, but looking farther down the road.

When carving long lines, try not to cut too deep. The more blade beneath the surface of the wood, the more friction or resistance you feel as you pull through the cut. A little resistance helps keep the cut smooth, but too much resistance has the opposite effect.

Also, when making long cuts consider the quality and direction of the grain. It is easier to make long, smooth cuts in a soft wood with relatively homogenous grain structure, like basswood, than in a wood with greater variation in grain density, like pine.

You can start with either horizontal or vertical lines. All cuts are made in First Position. Because a line is basically a long skinny rectangle, you have to sever the fibers at the ends of the line in order to fully relieve it from the wood. This can be done with a light plunge cut, or you can leave the waste attached until you carve an intersecting line—for example, if you carve the vertical lines first, the fibers at the very ends will be severed when you carve the horizontal lines.

4 The opposing cut relieves the line-chip.

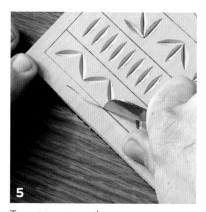

5 Try not to cut any deeper than necessary.

6 Chip-carve "lines" are simply long V-grooves; A narrow V-groove will be shallower than a wide one.

7

Make sure your knife is sharp before carving with the grain.

8

You want the blade to sever the fibers, not run with the grain.

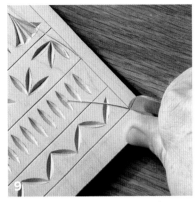

9

Carve all the way to the corner where the lines intersect.

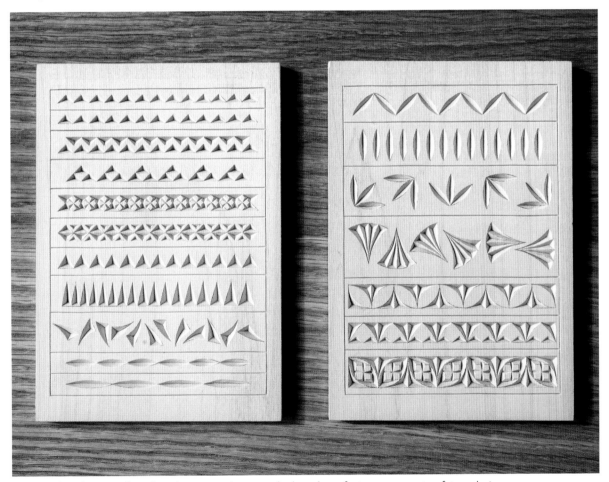

The completed practice boards make a convenient sampler board to refer to as you create a future designs..

4 FIRST PROJECTS

The repetition in practice boards is an excellent way to establish or touch up your technique. But to become a good carver there is simply no substitute for executing a piece of decorative carving from beginning to end. It's a little more high-stakes than carving a practice board, and it's where the really valuable and memorable lessons happen. In this chapter you'll use the skills and concepts you learned in the Practice Board Chapter, plus some new ones, such as batch cutting, carving circular border lines, and removing large chips in multiple layers.

TRIANGLE MOUNTAIN

These small plaques make great, quick warm up projects and are usually the first thing students in my classes carve when they move on from the practice boards. The design is an homage to one of the greatest art educators of the 20th century—the late, great Bob Ross. Happy little triangles.

BATCH CUTTING

Batch cutting is an efficient, and relatively speedy way to work through a group of chips that share the same or similar orientation to the grain by making all the cuts on one side of the chips in that group before turning the workpiece to make subsequent cuts. You can employ batch cutting, to some extent, when carving most of the projects in this chapter. The Triangle Mountain plaque is a good place to start, because it begins with batch cutting a group of chips with a very familiar shape.

I suggest dividing the design into groups of chips and carving one group at a time. Here I'm starting with the group of chips that form the mountain motif, making all of the First Position cuts for the group.

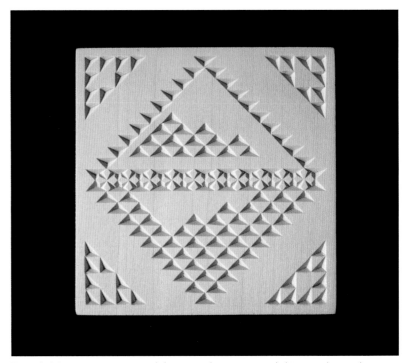

Triangle Mountain is composed the same three-cornered chips you learned to carve in the first four rows of Practice Board 1.

Batch cutting is an efficient way to work through a group of chips that share a common orientation to the grain.

Make all of the First Position cuts for a group of chips, then rotate the board and make all of the Second Position cuts for the same chips.

Finally, returning to the First Position knife grip, make all of the relief cuts for the group of chips.

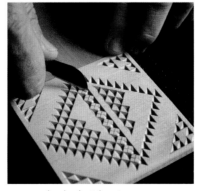

The notch cuts that define the stylized flowers can also be batch cut.

Next, rotate the board and make all of the Second Position cuts for that same group of chips. If you need a little extra real estate on which to rest your knuckle or thumb, use a scrap of equal thickness butted up against the side of your workpiece as a bracing board.

Now make all the relief cuts for the group of chips. Remember that there is no need to rotate the board for the relief cuts. It is a good idea to start by relieving the chip that is farthest away from you, and your way toward yourself so that you are always carving toward wood that is at least partially supported instead of carving toward already-carved chip pockets.

The notch chips that define the petals of the stylized flowers can also be batch cut. You can approach batch cutting in one of two ways here. You can make all the First Position cuts for one group of notches, then relieve those chips with a pass in Second Position. Alternately you can make the First Position cut followed by the Second Position cut, one notch at a time, all the way down the row of flowers. I prefer the first method because it means changing knife grip only once for a single batch of chips.

ASA-NO-HA

Two versions of the traditional Japanese Asa-No-Ha, or hemp leaf, pattern—the first example is built on a square grid, the second on a grid of hexagons—make good candidates for batch cutting, but with these patterns I prefer to alter my batch cutting approach a little. Instead of grouping chips by virtue of identical orientation to the grain, I break each pattern into "cells" and tackle one cell at a time

The cell for the square Asa-No-Ha pattern is a starburst shape composed of sixteen chips. I make one cut for each chip, toward the center of the starburst, turning the piece as I go. This is the first batch of cuts. The second batch of cuts is made from the center of the starburst out, on the opposite side of each chip, again turning the piece as I go, as indicated in the illustration. The final step is to make the relief cuts for all the chips in the cell. Once I carve all the cells, I remove the surrounding chips.

This version of the asa-no-ha pattern is based on a square grid.

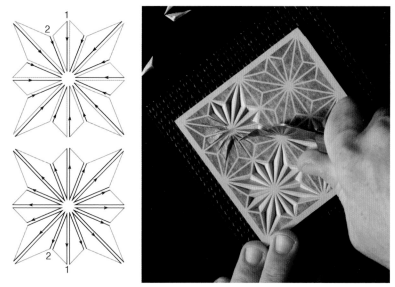

The batch cut sequence I use for the square asa-no-ha pattern.

Both the square and hexagonal asa-no-ha patterns look great in directional light that throws the grid patterns into stark contrast.

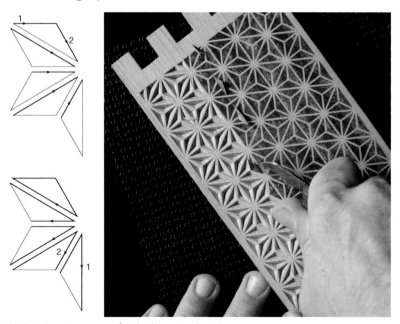

The batch cut sequence for the hexagonal-grid.

Because of the way the hexagonal Asa-No-ha pattern repeats, I prefer to break the pattern into asymmetrical cells that stack, as opposed to starburst-shaped cells as in the square Asa-No-Ha. The starburst approach is also an option with the hexagonal asa-no-ha, so you may want to try it too. Either approach will work—this is simply my personal preference.

The sequence of cuts follows the same logic regardless of which approach you take to breaking the pattern into cells: outside-in along one side of each chip in the cell, inside-out along the opposite side of each chip, followed by relief cuts. Before starting the next row of cells, carve the row of chips that separate the rows.

TULIP POT

The first cuts for this batch of chips are made with the grain.

Next, make all the curved cuts.

Finally, relieve the chips by carving across the grain. This process is identical to rows 16 & 17 of the practice boards.

For the chips that define the leaves of the stylized tulips, I carve the lines that run with the grain first, followed by the curved lines around the leaves, finally relieving the chips by carving across the grain. Notice how I've organized the batch cutting approach here—all the chips with identical grain orientation are carved as a group. For these chips I'm making all my cuts in First Position.

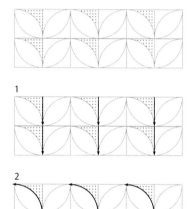

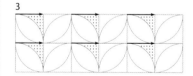

THE SEED OF LIFE

The first batch of cuts for this version of the Seed of Life are made across the grain.

The chip-removal sequences for the Seed of Life when carving only the two-cornered chips.

Roll the angle of cut up a bit at the end of the relief cut to prevent excessive undercutting of the surrounding wood.

This is an ancient pattern. The oldest known examples of it dates to the 6th or 7th century BCE in Assyria (what is now northern Iraq). At some point it exploded into the ornamental vocabulary of wood, stone and metal workers across Europe and the near and middle east. There are many, many variations of the interlocking circle grid; It has been used all around the world and even today remains a common decorative motif. This simple iteration, sometimes referred to as the Seed Of Life (another version with nineteen inter-locking circles is often called the Flower Of Life) has been used by chip carvers in wood for centuries and illustrates how some designs can be carved in multiple ways—in this case you can carve the two-cornered chips, the three-cornered chips, or both.

TWO-CORNERED CHIPS & CIRCULAR BORDER LINE

Batch cutting can be used when carving all three versions of the Seed Of Life. The two-cornered-chip-only version can be neatly divided into three groups of chips with identical orientation to the grain. For each batch of chips, make all the cuts on one side of the two-cornered chips, then flip the piece around for the relief cuts.

THE SEED OF LIFE (CONTINUED)

Adding a circular border should be done last and in two continuous First Position cuts. The first cut is made with the edge of the knife facing away from the center of the pattern. Start the cut at the point where the line is parallel to the grain. As you pull through the cut, turn the workpiece gradually to keep cutting. Use a scrap of wood the thickness of the workpiece as a thumb brace if needed.

The second cut is made with the edge of the knife facing the center of the pattern. Again, start the cut parallel to the grain. It's easy to tense up when carving borders like this. Try not to grip the knife too tightly—you'll get a smoother cut if you stay relaxed.

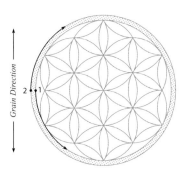

Carving the circular border of the two-cornered chip Seed of Life. Make the first cut with the knife angled away from the center of the pattern.

The relief cut for the circular border is made with the knife angled toward the center of the pattern.

Batch cuts for the three-cornered chip Seed of Life. I left the waste in the bottom of the chip pockets and then cleaned them all up by repeating my cuts as necessary.

I ordered my batch cuts so that the relief cuts are made across the grain.

THREE-CORNERED CHIPS

The three-cornered chip Seed Of Life can also be batch cut. First, remove one set of three-cornered chips, followed by the group oriented in the opposite direction. Finally cut the three-cornered border chips that on the edges of the pattern.

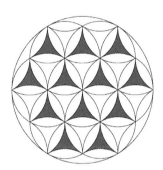

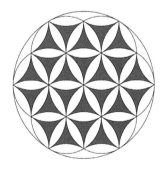

The chip-removal sequence for the three-cornered chip Seed of Life.

DRAWING THE SEED OF LIFE

The Seed Of Life can be drawn using two compass settings—one setting to draw the interlocking circles that form the pattern, and a second setting (twice the length of the first) to bound it. Starting with the smaller setting, draw a circle. Wherever you place the point of the compass for this first circle will be the center of your Seed Of Life. Next, place the compass point somewhere along the circumference of the first circle and draw another circle. Take note that the location of the second circle will determine the orientation of the chips in the Seed Of Life pattern to the direction of the grain. For ease of carving, I suggest orienting the pattern so that none of the two-cornered chips are oriented perfectly parallel to the grain. Every new circle will give you new compass point locations. Fill out the entire pattern, reset your compass, and draw the boundary line. Finally, erase all the unneeded lines outside and inside the boundary.

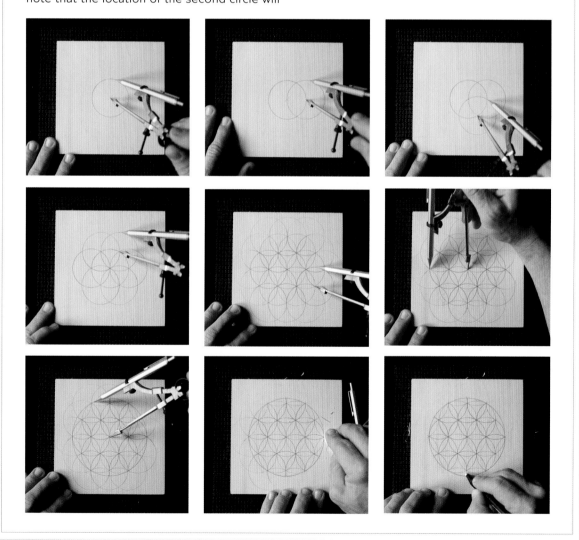

When carving the Seed of Life in full, I prefer to progress one row of chips at a time across the pattern.

Working across the pattern one row of chips at a time means having to turn the piece more often. The advantage is that you can always begin carving a new row of chips with the knife directed away from the chip pockets you have already carved.

SEED OF LIFE CARVED IN FULL

To remove all the chips of the Seed Of Life, I prefer working across the pattern—left to right, or right to left, either way works— removing the chips in vertical rows. Some amount of batch cutting is still possible in this scenario, as the photographs at left show.

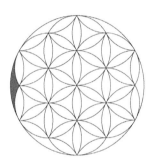

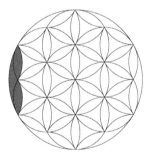

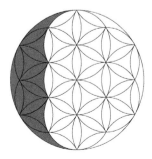

THE SEED OF LIFE (CONTINUED)

Paint is a nice touch for some carvings, especially simple designs like the Minimalist Flowers. The process for painting the flowers is covered in the Finishing chapter.

MINIMALIST FLOWERS

Carving a test piece gives you an opportunity to identify problem areas and practice the challenging parts of a pattern like the tight curves around the flower petals.

I keep my strop and strop compound nearby while carving. It's a good idea to strop your knife every so often to keep the edge fresh. I usually strop every half hour or so of carving.

For the center of the second flower, the first cut of each chip should made with the knife pointed away from the previous chip.

A simple design does not always make for easy carving. In fact, sometimes simple designs are the most challenging to carve cleanly because they leave nowhere for mistakes or irregularities to hide.

It's a good idea to carve a test piece before tackling a particularly challenging project. I do this often. It helps me warm up and get in touch with the fine motor skills it takes to control the knife. It also allows me to identify problem spots in the carving and plan my approach to carving the real thing. Before carving this flower on the shelf, I practiced the flower head portion on scrap wood. I've carved this pattern before, and I knew that I needed a practice session first— carving the intersecting lines that define the flower petals without blowing out the points is tricky.

As you near the center of the flower head, roll your cutting angle up a bit to prevent the tip of the knife from slipping too far under the wood that forms the tips of the adjacent petal. As you pull the knife around the tight curve that defines bulbous end of the petals, tip the handle up to reduce the amount of the blade in the cut. to carve the center of the second flower head, the first cut of each chip should be made with the knife edge facing away from the previously carved chip.

COW'S NOSE

Here we have another extremely old pattern composed of a grid of interlocking circles. The pattern dates back to ancient Mesopotamia where it was used in Babylonian mathematics and geometry, and was known as the apsamikkum, which translates roughly to "the opening of the lyre" or, oddly, the "cow's nose." Like the Seed Of Life pattern, it has been a staple of the ornamental design vocabulary of European carvers since at least the middle ages.

My preferred order of chip removal for the Cow's Nose is to carve all the chips in the central square first, working my way around counterclockwise (do it clockwise if you're a lefty), and then proceeding to carve the remaining chips from the central square out to the edges.

The Cow's Nose carved in the Honduras mahogany lid of a small ceramic vessel made by ceramicist Emily Webb.

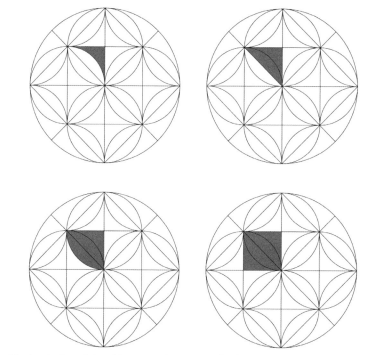

The beginning of the chip removal sequence for the Cow's Nose.

Working through the chips in a circular direction allows the first cut for each chip to be made with the knife facing away from the already-carved chip pockets.

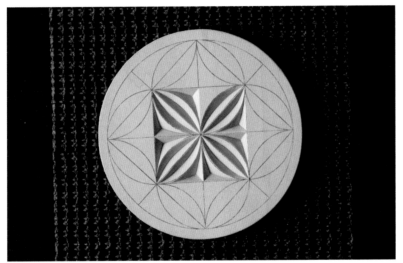

The final chip leaves you no choice but to carve toward one of the surrounding chip pockets.

Because the chip is oriented with the grain, the risk of causing damage by carving toward the adjacent chip pockets is reduced.

By now, you know that it is best to carve away from previously carved chip pockets whenever possible. It is especially important to direct cuts away from unsupported short-grain. However, removing the chips of the central square in circular order means that will eventually have no choice but to carve toward unsupported wood. You can minimize the risk of disaster on the final chip by making a strategic choice: Start with a chip that has a wall running with the grain.

Doing this means that the first cut made on the final chip will be directed toward a relatively strong long-grain chip wall. Once the chips of the central square are removed, you can then carve all the remaining chips without ever making a first-cut toward unsupported short grain.

CHARLES HAYWARD BOX

I ran across this design through Lost Art Press's republication of the writings of Charles Hayward. It's tiny but it carries a valuable lesson: how to carve extra large chips. This pattern is a good example of one that should be practiced on a piece of scrap before attempting to execute it on a box lid or other decorative application. The process of removing large chips is straightforward but, of course, takes some practice.

A good rule of thumb for carving larger chips is to keep your angle of cut lower than average. It's hard to say exactly how much, because everyone carves at a slightly different angle. The larger the surface area of a chip, the deeper its center will be. Chips with deep centers are hard to remove cleanly, and their centers disappear into the shadows cast by the walls of the chip pocket. You will have a much easier time carving large chips and produce a more balanced looking carving if you keep the angle low.

The first step, show here on one of the large three cornered chips, is to make your cuts as you normally would, though with your cutting angle cheated down a bit more than usual. You will probably find that the chip does not release from the wood, though you might be able to wiggle it a bit. Do not

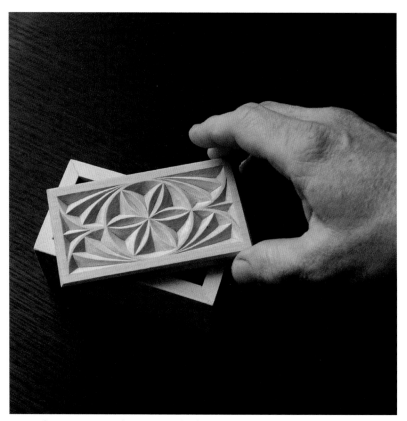

Large chips are removed in stages. The first step is to make cuts along each side of the chip. The size of the chip means that these cuts will be pulling cuts.

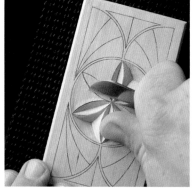

The first series of cuts frees the upper half of the chip, which breaks off, leaving waste in the bottom of the chip pocket.

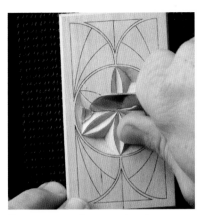

Remove waste by repeating the cuts. The side of the knife tracks against the facets created by the first cuts.

The same process applies to two-cornered chips.

try to pry it out! Instead, repeat all of your cuts, trying to achieve the same angle as before. It may take a few repetitions, but eventually the top half of the chip will break free.

Now repeat your sequence of cuts once again. Maintain the same lowered angle of cut, but try not to remove any additional material from the walls of the chip pocket. Repeat the sequence of cuts until the remainder of the waste pops free.

REMOVING PATTERN LINES

Pattern lines can be removed by sanding very lightly with a fresh piece of 220 sandpaper wrapped around a block. A block with a tiny bit of give works well, so here I'm using an extra strop I had on hand—a piece of wood with leather glued to one side. Sand lightly so as not to damage your work. For more delicate carvings, you can get the lines off with a sand eraser. These are available at most art supply stores and they are exactly what they sound like: a rubber eraser embedded with sand.

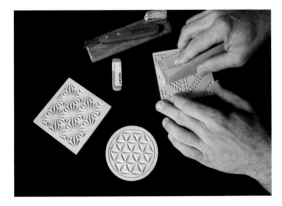

5 COMPOUND CHIPS & LETTERING

In previous chapters you have encountered a few simple examples of compound chip shapes (row 19 of the practice boards) and intersecting chips (the border lines from the practice boards and the Tulip Pot project). The technical principles presented in this chapter will help you make clean work of a wide variety similar challenges, including carved letters.

COMPOUND CHIPS

This example board contains a few motifs that are representative of both compound chip shapes and intersecting chip shapes. The distinction between "compound" and "intersecting" chip shapes is somewhat semantic—they both consist of complex carved shapes which are usually best carved by breaking the complex shape down into simpler shapes that can be removed in stages.

The three symbols (the five pointed star is shown in two different orientations to the grain direction) are examples of what I call compound chip shapes: each one is a carved representation of a single shape. The gridded box that contains them is a carved representation of multiple intersecting lines.

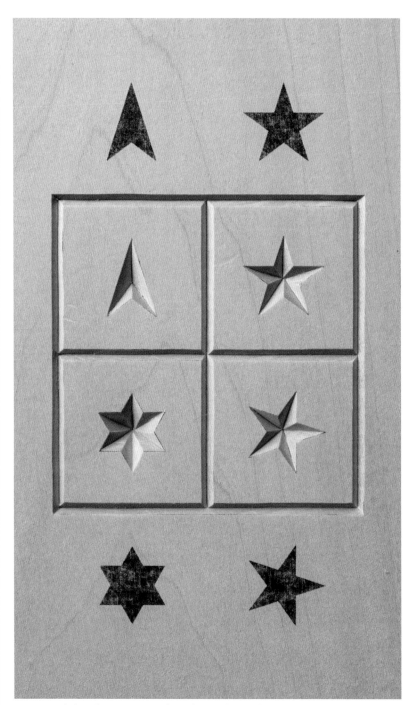

Compound chip shapes practice board carved, and the shapes (in black) they are intended to represent.

The compound chip shapes practice board before carving. The shapes are drawn to illustrate where each cut happens.

"But," you might say, "the gridded box is also a single shape!" I can't say that you're wrong about that. I can only point you to my previous caveat (semantics, etc.) and tell you that they are useful categories for describing a chip carving pattern in terms of what it is meant to represent. So with apologies to anyone who finds it irksome, I'll stick to this nomenclature for the time being.

The first step to carving a compound shape is to break it up into simpler, constituent chip shapes. For angular polygons like the ones shown on the example board, that almost always means a series of three-cornered chips and notch chips. Once you get the hang of the concept, it's easy enough to do in your minds eye, but for the sake of clarity I've drawn each compound shape as a series of intersecting lines that indicate where the necessary cuts must happen.

ARROW

We'll start with the arrow shape. It's the simplest of the compound shapes pictured and a good introduction to the process. The arrow breaks down into two triangles, or one large three-cornered chip and a notch chip. The first cut is made from the bottom left corner all the way to the top point of the arrow.

Now turn the board and make a cut from the top point of the arrow down to the bottom right corner. To remove the large three-cornered chip, turn the board again and cut from the bottom right corner, all the way across to the opposite side of the arrow.

Two sides of the small remaining triangle have already been cut, so a single press cut relieves the chip. The press cut is made with the edge of the knife, rather than the tip. As you press the knife down, follow the remaining line and aim for the tip of the knife to land in the center of the arrow-shaped chip pocket. Despite the difference in scale, this maneuver essentially the same as the cuts used for notching out the petals of the stylized flowers in the practice board, rows 5 and 18.

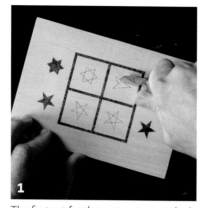

The first cut for the arrow starts at the bottom point and finishes at the top point, with the edge of the blade facing the middle of the shape. The second cut starts where the first cut ended.

The third cut removes the larger of the two chips that make up the arrow shape. Next, remove the smaller chip by pressing the blade into the line.

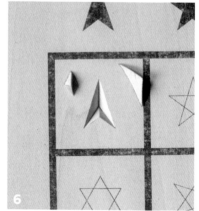

Because the other two sides of the smaller chip have already been cut, it only takes one cut to remove the smaller chip.

FIVE-POINTED STAR 1

Each cut starts at one point of the star and continues across the shape to the opposite point. All cuts are made with the edge of the blade facing toward the center of the shape.

The third, fourth and fifth cuts will cross the cuts you have already made.

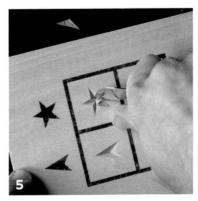

If there's waste left in the bottom of the star-shaped chip pocket, remove it the same way you would for any chip: repeat your cuts until all the fibers holding the waste in place are severed.

The process is similar for the five pointed stars. Start at the bottom left corner of the star and make a full depth cut up to the top point. The next cut starts where the previous cut ended, and so on and so on, chasing the lines clockwise all the way around the star, repositioning the board as necessary for each cut. It may take a little practice to get your depth of cut just right for these, (and depth of cut will, of course, depend on the size of the star.)

Why this particular order of cut? Go back and look at the photo of the first cut for the first five-pointed star. Note that the knife is traveling against the grain relative to the workpiece side of the cut—the side where the chip pocket facets will be. Making the against-the-grain cut first, when all the fibers are locked in place, helps achieve clean facets on that side of the chip pocket. If you were to make the same cut as the last one in the sequence, you would be much more likely to end up with rough, chattery facets.

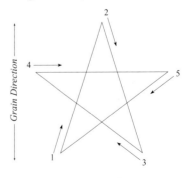

FIVE-POINTED STAR 2

Now, what is the best place to start on the second five-pointed star? The shape is identical, but it is rotated 90° in relation to the direction of the grain. Notice my first cut, once again, is made against the grain (in relation to the workpiece, not the chip, which will soon be waste), and then I follow the lines around the star as before.

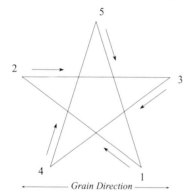

SIX-POINTED STAR

The six-pointed star is comparatively simple. The star breaks up neatly into two equal-sized equilateral triangles superimposed on one another. Remove one of the equilateral triangles, then notch out each of the remaining points of the star with a First Position press cut, followed by a Second Position press cut.

The second five-pointed star is different only in it's orientation to the grain. The cuts are made in the same way—start at one point, carve across to the opposite point.

Once again, the third, fourth and fifth cuts will cross the first two cuts.

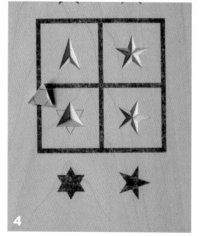

The six-pointed star is removed in stages, by first carving a large equilateral triangular chip and then removing notch chips for the other three star points.

GRIDDED BOX

 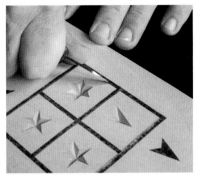

Chip carved "lines" are v-shaped grooves. Each line is removed with two opposing cuts. This is another situation where cuts will cross one another.

For V-groove lines that intersect at corners, be sure to extend your cuts all the way into the corner.

For cuts that begin where a V-groove has already been removed, start with the knife's tip in the existing V-groove.

Treat these two segments as a single V-groove line, cutting directly across the wood that has already been carved away.

The "lines" that make up the gridded box are of course, technically speaking, actually a series of intersecting V-grooves carved with long, pulling cuts in First Position. The order of cuts is not as crucial in this situation, but carving the cross-grain lines first is generally a good idea. Think of the gridded box as two sets of three lines crossing one another. Each cut passes through all three of the intersecting lines, from one side of the box to the other.

To carve a line that intersects with the grooves you've already carved, start your cuts with the tip of the knife down in the V-groove and carve directly across intersecting grooves in one long pass, from end to end.

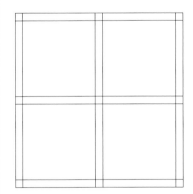

THE KELLS GRID

This pattern was adapted from a small panel on a page in the 9th century illuminated manuscript the Book of Kells. Some time after I found and adapted this pattern for chip carving, I ran across images of a medieval church in Ireland with a virtually identical pattern carved into the stonework. I do not know which direction the lines of influence ran in the 9th century—whether artists working in two dimensions would have been influenced by the stone carvers of the time, or perhaps the other way around. Either way, I was pleased to learn that I was not the first person who had decided it made a good carving pattern.

At first glance it is quite eye-popping, and the way the pattern works can be hard to parse visually, however the grid is composed of a simple repeating cell (with some variations around the edges of the panel) that interlocks with its neighboring repetitions. It can be broken down into a collection of intersecting three-cornered chips and V-groove chips.

The Kells Grid applied to a small coin-bank in stained butternut wood.

The repetition of the Kells Grid is easier to understand when it is broken up into repeating "cells."

This illustration shows how the cell can be broken up into its constituent chips.

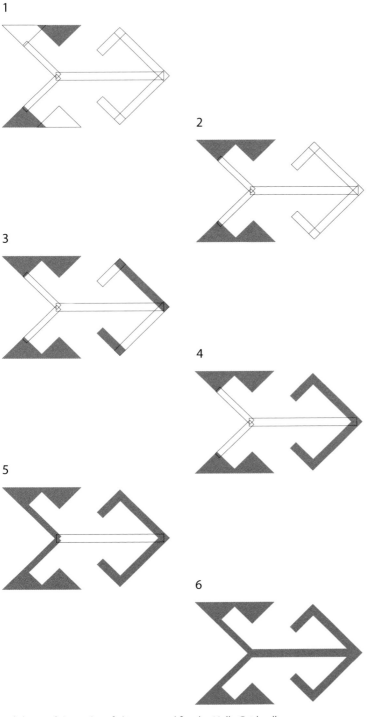

1

2

3

4

5

6

A breakdown of the order of chip removal for the Kells Grid cells.

I typically default to carving in First Position, and stick with it whenever I can because it offers the greatest amount of stability and control, and by using a single position, the angle of cut achieved from facet to facet is more likely to be consistent. Given the constraint of carving exclusively in First Position (and being right handed—sorry again lefties, the following sequence will be mirror imaged for you) here is a breakdown of the order in which I remove the chips of each cell.

While a roadmap of which chips to remove in which order may certainly be useful, it will be of much greater benefit in the long run for you to understand the logic that determines the ordering. As I have mentioned many times before (and will continue to mention), the orientation of a given chip, or collection of chips, to the direction of the grain is what drives those decisions.

THE KELLS GRID (CONTINUED)

For a carving to look as clean and crisp as possible, the points of uncarved wood formed by intersecting chip pockets and V-grooves must also be crisp and clean. The primary areas of concern are the points composed of cross-grain wood (also known as short-grain) because they are especially weak and susceptible to breakage.

Even the slight friction and wedging action created by the knife as it passes one of these weak spots can cause the fibers to separate from one another. This is a problem; If the weak cross-grain point has already been excessively undercut from one or both sides, and the fibers are then pulled apart by the drag of the knife, it is likely to break or crumble away entirely, leaving a stubby or jagged protuberance that spoils the crispness of the intersection and distracts from the overall rhythm of the pattern.

Clean carving is essential for the Kells Grid to have the greatest visual impact, so the corners formed by intersecting chips must be clean and sharp.

The corners marked in red indicate potential problem spots—corners of uncarved wood made up of "short grain" are easily broken or damaged. This can be mitigated by carefully ordering the cuts used to remove the chips around those corners.

With one chip removed (the shaded triangle) the first cut for the adjacent triangular chip should be made in the indicated direction. Keep in mind that this scenario will be mirrored for left-handed carvers.

In the case of the Kells Grid cell, there are a couple approaches you can take to decrease the likelihood of damaging the weak cross-grain points. One simple solution is to remove the shaded chips first, then remove the intersecting chips, beginning with the indicated direction of cut. (This is the approach I have taken in the photographs.) Take special note of the cut in terms of grain direction: with the knife traveling in the direction indicated, any friction or drag created by the knife will compress rather than separate the fibers of the cross-grain point.

In these pics you can see that I am employing batch cutting to make the Kells Grid move along with minimal turning and repositioning.

With all the triangular chips on one side of the Kells Grid cells removed, repeat the process on the opposite side of the cells.

THE KELLS GRID (CONTINUED)

Another approach is to carve both chips in tandem with the following sequence of cuts. If you choose this option be sure to temporarily decrease your depth of cut as you pass the cross-grain point so as not to undercut it excessively.

You can apply the same principle of ordering your cuts to protect relatively weak short-grain in other parts of the Kells Grid pattern, as well as many other situations—we'll encounter this again in the following sections on carving letters.

After removing all triangular chips, begin removing the intersecting V-groove lines.

This part of the pattern can be also batch cut. I prefer to cut all the lines on one side of the cells first, then the lines on the opposite side of the cells.

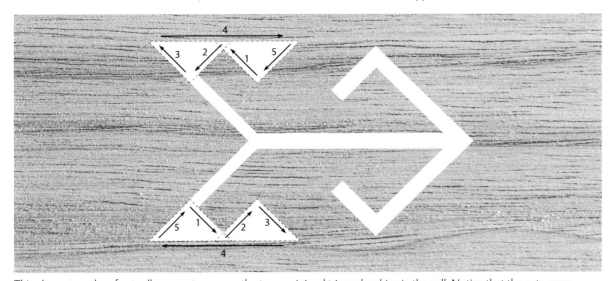

This alternate order of cuts allows you to remove the two conjoined triangular chips in the cell. Notice that the cuts move around the shape in a circular manner.

LETTERING

I prefer to "teach someone to fish" rather than "give them a fish." In other words, I try to provide a thorough understanding of the principles and techniques that yield clean carving rather than merely hand you a carve-by-number roadmap and say "Just do it this way." Rote, step-by-step direction is valuable, especially for beginners, but to progress in any handcraft it becomes necessary to learn the logic behind the how-to. So, instead of doing a tedious (and less valuable) cut-by-cut breakdown of every character in the two alphabets, I focus on a few characters from each that best illustrate concepts applicable to carving letters and other shapes.

Letterforms are composed of strokes, and the strokes of chip carved letters are often rendered as V-groove lines. Brushed or inked strokes overlap to form a given character, but the V-grooves of carved letters intersect in a variety of ways: Strokes meet at corners, cross one another, or one terminates in the middle of another. Many letterforms in our own alphabet have three or four V-grooved stroke segments radiating from a shared point. You can probably see what I'm driving at: in order to carve letters cleanly, you must learn to carve the intersections of V-grooves cleanly. That is where the runes come in.

The play of light and shadow in carved letters serves the roll that ink does in printed type, it is therefore very important to keep your carving as clean as possible when carving letters, so as not to create visual distractions from the form of the letter.

THE ELDER FUTHARK RUNES

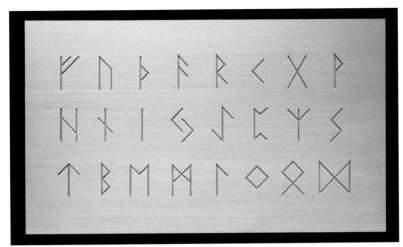

The Elder Futhark runes make an excellent exercise for learning to carve intersecting V-groove lines without the added difficulty of curves and changes in line width.

The | character requires four cuts: Two long cuts along each side and two small plunge cuts at both ends of the stroke. The plunge cuts at the terminating points of strokes can be made at any time.

Whenever possible, I prefer to work exclusively in First Position because it offers greater stability and control. This is especially true for the long cuts employed in carving letter characters.

The Elder Futhark runic alphabet was a writing system used by various Germanic people groups between the 2nd and 10th centuries. If my choice to include them here seems odd, consider what they offer purely as carving exercises in the context of this chapter: Intersecting chips galore, many of them are similar to arrangements you will find in our own alphabet, but without complicating factors such as the curves and serifs you will encounter in the Roman Capitals later on.

FIRST POSITION STOP & OVERLAPPING CUTS

First, a few general technical notes. Whenever possible I carve in First Position because it allows for greater stability and control than Second Position, therefore all of the following instructions are organized around that preference.

The rune patterns as I've rendered them here (there are many aesthetic variations of the runes) are composed of straight strokes of equal width and simple square terminations. The cut for a termination point is made with a small plunge cut which can be carved at any time (it really doesn't matter when you do it), and so I have not worked them into my discussion about cut order.

THE ELDER FUTHARK RUNES (CONTINUED)

In order for two V-groove lines to intersect cleanly, each cut must fully cross whatever line it intersects with, sometimes overlapping other cuts before the chips are fully removed. For characters printed in a solid color (or merely outlined) on the wood, this means eyeballing where your cuts begin and end.

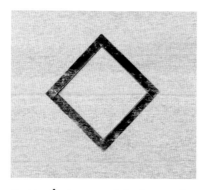 

For the ◇ character all the lines on the inside of the character are carved first and each cut overlaps its adjacent cuts.

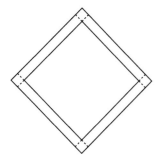

When making a cut that extends from a V-groove that has already been carved, start with the knife situated fully within the V-groove, with the tip of the knife resting at the bottom of the groove.

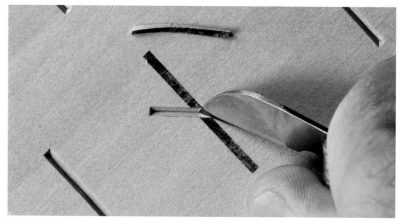

The vertical stroke can be removed either by carving directly across the diagonal stroke, treating it like a single unbroken chip, or by carving one side first and then the other. For the second approach, begin the cut with the tip of the knife resting in the bottom of the diagonal stroke's chip pocket.

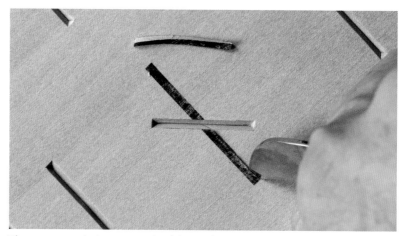

The cut proceeds down one side of the stroke segment.

Note the grain direction here. In this orientation to the grain, the (Γ) character presents a focused lesson on how ordering your cuts can help you protect the weak short-grain points on the inside of line intersections from breakage.

SHORT-GRAIN POINTS

Every pair of intersecting V-grooves forms at least one point, and because wood grain is stronger in one direction than it is in the other, points that cross the grain (short-grain points) are relatively weak and easily damaged in the process of carving. As I discussed in the section on the Kells Grid, the best way to protect weak short-grain points is by carefully ordering your cuts and controlling your depth of cut to prevent excessive undercutting.

This bears repeating because in many cases the points found in carved letter characters are formed by acute angles, meaning that they are long, delicate and therefore exceptionally prone to damage from to reckless carving.

The character Γ with its single, sharp short-grain point is a good place to start. How can you order your cuts to prevent the drag and wedging action of the knife from separating the short-grain fibers of the point? The answer, as stated in the Kells Grid section, is to make the cut that could otherwise cause the damage first, while all of the fibers are locked in place by surrounding wood. This can be restated as a general rule of thumb: If possible, the first cut should be made alongside the point, in the direction the point is pointing.

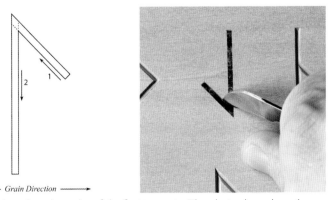

Grain Direction

The diagram describes the order of the first two cuts. The photo shows how the first of the two cuts are executed.

THE ELDER FUTHARK RUNES (CONTINUED)

Now, where to make the second cut? There isn't always a single best answer, but in this case the choice is clear, and can also be stated as a follow-up rule of thumb: If possible the second cut should be made along the other side of the point, opposite the direction the point is pointing.

Now that the short-grain point has been defined by the first two cuts, all that remains is to relieve the chips with the other necessary cuts. It's still important to be careful: try to cut only as deep as is necessary, especially around the point. Excessive undercutting could still cause damage and chip-out.

CARVING THE ᛗ RUNE

Now let's apply our rules of thumb to a slightly more complex character, this time one with a very familiar shape. With the grain running horizontally, the ᛗ confronts us with three short-grain points. Take a look at a diagram of the character with all of the cuts articulated—which cuts should you make first to ensure the cleanest result?

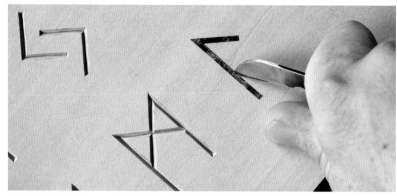

The order of cuts, and the second cut in practice.

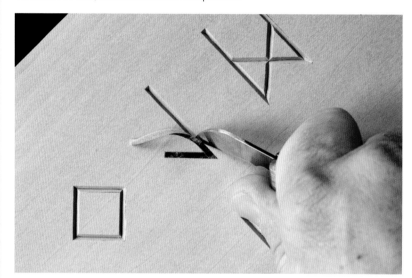

The remaining cuts are then made to remove the chips.

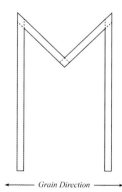

The ᛗ character has three short-grain points to navigate. The diagram shows how the cuts overlap.

Grain Direction

 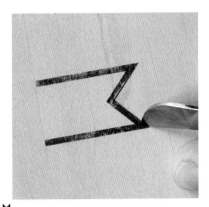

The first and second cuts for carving the M

The third cut for the M character.

The first rule states that the first cut should be made alongside the short-grain point, and in the same direction that the point is pointing. The M gives us no choice but to bend that rule a little because either set of two adjacent short-grain points are situated on opposite sides of the same chip; making the best possible cut for one point means making a less than optimal first cut for its neighbor. In a situation like this, careful control of the knife—especially controlling the depth of cut—will make all the difference.

Even when there is no single best solution, there are usually one or two sequences that are better than others. Try this one, and as you carve pay attention to how the prescribed order of cuts satisfies the requirements of the two rules of thumb.

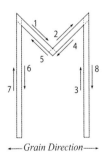

←—Grain Direction—→

This diagram illustrates the order of cuts. Try to understand the principle behind the way the cuts are ordered: the second cut alongside a short-grain point should be in the direction that will *compress* the fibers of the point instead of potentially pulling them apart or encouraging breakage.

THE ELDER FUTHARK RUNES (CONTINUED)

You are probably getting the hang of this by now, but let's take a look at one more character with a step-by-step diagram. The ᛉ is another familiar shape with three short-grain points. Like many letterforms, there are multiple order-of-cut sequences that will work for this character. Carve through this sequence and, again, notice how the sequence of cuts helps to isolate the short-grain points from damage.

I'll go through this one step by step. Cuts 1 and 2 are made alongside and in the direction of the upper and lower short-grain points—all the wood fibers are locked in place, eliminating any possibility of the knife drag causing damage. Cut 3 defines one side of the vertical stroke while also serving as the second defining cut for the upper and lower short-grain points as well as the first defining cut for the middle point. Cut 4 relieves the chip that forms the vertical stroke. While Cut 4 could be made later in the sequence, removing the vertical chip at this point provides better visibility of the tip of the knife during cuts 5, 7, and 8.

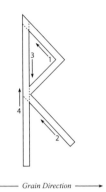

Grain Direction

The eight cuts needed (not including the small plunge cuts for stroke terminations) to carve the ᛉ character. Follow the diagram but try to internalize the logic of the order of operations.

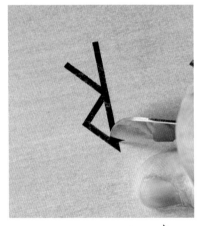

The first and second cuts for the ᛉ can be made without turning the workpiece.

With the third and fourth cuts, the first V-groove chip is cut free from the wood.

The sixth cut for the ᚱ. Intersecting chips, by definition, share fibers with one another where they intersect. Because of this they will often stay attached until the adjacent chips are removed.

Cuts 5 and 6 relieve the "leg" and the upper chip (in the photo this chip stays put because it is till attached at the other end—cuts 7 and 8 will relieve it fully.)

Cut 7 starts with the tip of the knife down in the bottom of the V-groove of the vertical stroke, and is the second defining cut of the middle short-grain point—following our second rule of thumb, the cut progresses alongside that point but in the opposite direction. Cut 8 relieves the chip. Then any remaining waste is cleaned up.

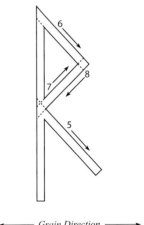

Grain Direction

The seventh and eighth cuts remove the final chip, and in the process the previously carved chip is also freed.

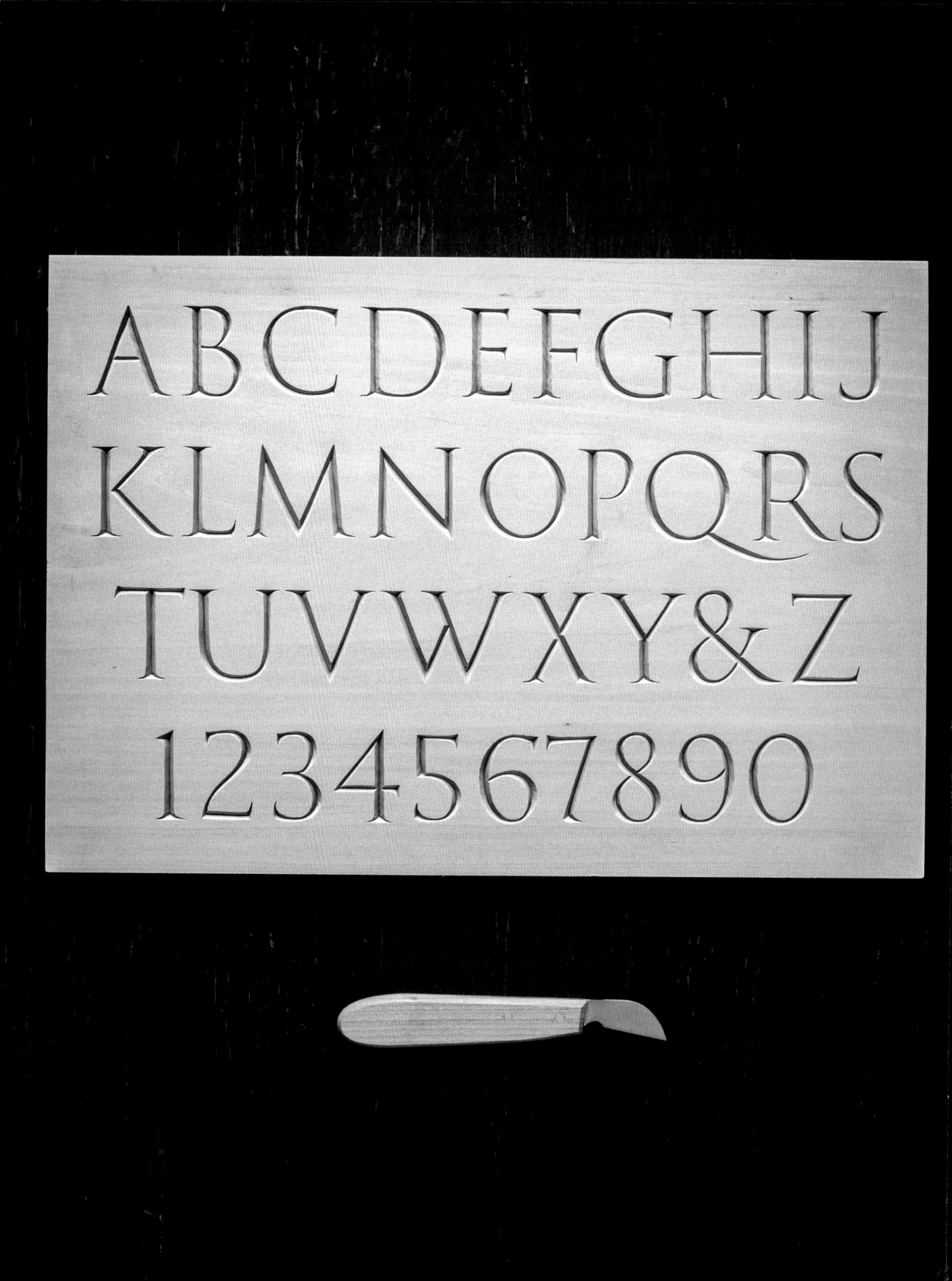
ABCDEFGHIJ
KLMNOPQRS
TUVWXY&Z
1234567890

ROMAN CAPITALS

The order-of-cut logic explained in the previous section is applied to the Roman capital A. The first cut runs along side the short-grained point at the top of the A, the second cut is made on the opposite side, in the direction that is less likely to stress the short-grain point.

Like the small plunge cuts used in the runes, the stroke terminations for the capitals can be carved at any time.

The cuts for the various strokes of the character overlap.

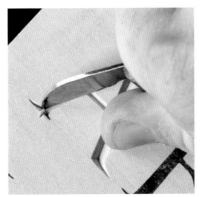

The serifs can be carved as part of the stroke in one continuous cut, or notched out after the body of the character has been carved.

The Roman capitals that I present here are my own redrawings of the letterforms in Edward M. Catich's magnificent book The Origin of the Serif. Catich's Roman capitals were derived from his study of ancient Roman inscriptions in stone, specifically the inscription known as the Trajan Inscription, long held to be the quintessential example of Roman capitals. Roman letter writers left their mark on the world, so to speak, and the influence of the style is everywhere to be seen in the world of typography, from newspapers to contemporary handcarved signs and monuments. The principles of chip carving clean intersections I laid out for the Elder Futhark runes hold true for the Roman alphabet, but the Roman letters posses several distinctive traits that require special attention. First, let's talk about serifs.

Serifs are a slight projection finishing off the stroke of a letter and are a defining characteristic of Roman lettering. (Catich famously asserted that letters in ancient Rome were brushed onto stone before being carved, and that the serif is an aesthetic product of this technical sequence.) The serifs of carved letters can be dealt with in two ways, depending on their size, shape and orientation to the rest of a character. Some serifs may be carved as part of a long

ROMAN CAPITALS (CONTINUED)

continuous cut made on one side of a stroke, while others may be easier to remove via small notch cuts made after the larger chips have been carved away. This is, to a degree, a matter of preference, as well as your personal level of comfort with making tightly curved cuts. For most of the Roman letters I prefer to remove the serifs separately and last.

The V-grooves representing strokes in my version of the Elder Futhark runes were all of the same width. The Roman letters, on the other hand, contain a great deal of variation, often within a single stroke. In many cases two grooves of differing widths intersect and the difference should be taken into account when carving. As you know by now, given that all your cuts are made at a constant angle: the larger the surface area of a chip, the deeper it will be. Hence, the H's horizontal groove is only about half the depth of the vertical grooves. The lesson: don't carve any deeper than you need to.

With the R we have the inverse situation—the wide-ish leg of the R emerges from a relatively narrow point of the R's lobe (the big round part). I've found this type of intersection looks best if you lower your angle of cut just a tiny bit on the wider groove.

V-grooves of different widths, when carved using the same angle of cut, will necessarily have different depths. When a narrower/shallower V-groove intersects with a wider/deeper groove, the difference in depth should be evident at the point of intersection.

For the inverse scenario where a wide V-groove intersects with a narrower one, lower your angle of cut for the wider V-groove line. This will cause the wider groove to be a little less deep and create a cleaner visual effect at the point of intersection.

For the capital O, cut the outside line of the character first. This is the opposite of the way you would approach a circular border on a rosette, but it makes sense here: there is no carving within the circular V-groove of the O to protect from chipping out.

Cutting the interior line of the O character second gives you another slight advantage in the way of cleanliness—because the outside line was carved first, any splitting caused by the wedging action of the blade is likely to be "captured" within the character instead of running into the wood around the character.

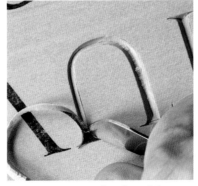

A similar order of operations is used for the U—cut the exterior line first. If the blade runs with the grain on the curve, the split will be captured within the lines of the character.

The Roman letters contain many technical challenges, but the thing that seems to really intimidate a lot of carvers is the curves. I get it. They are challenging, indeed. Here are a few tips to help you navigate them successfully.

For the O (and the Q and the 0), cut the outside line first. If the grain is oriented horizontally, begin your cut at the top or bottom of the character, just slightly ahead of the apex of the curve. If the grain is oriented vertically, begin your cut at a corresponding spot on the side of the character. Cut all the way around to where you started. Tip the knife up on its blade axis to help prevent chatter as you cut, but try to keep your angle of cut consistent.

Now make the second cut, starting at the inside apex of the curve, cutting all the way around. Don't worry about waste left behind in the chip pocket. Sometimes it is easier to make a long, smooth curved cut if the depth of cut is a little shallower, even if it means leaving behind some waste. You can go back and clean that up after the fact.

On the U, the same as with the O, cut the outside line first. When you make the inside cut—the relief cut—the chip may split (or not!) as the cut approaches the long grain, but the split will be "captured" by the curve.

ROMAN CAPITALS (CONTINUED)

And lastly, the ampersand and the 8. What can I say about the ampersand and the 8? They are hard! There's no way around it: Practice, practice, practice. I suggest trying following sequences:

1

2

3

4

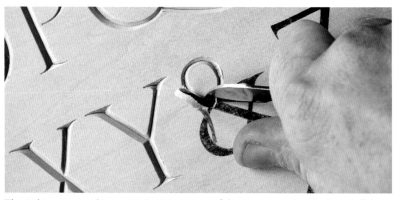

The tight curves and two crossing V-grooves of the ampersand make it one of the more difficult characters to carve. Try removing the chips in the order I've suggested and remember to keep your knife tipped up a bit as you round the curves.

The second chip removed in ampersand is the tail.

Carve carefully across the already-carved V-groove of the tail and proceed onto the final chip.

The final cut terminates in V-groove of the tail. Be gentle as you finish up this cut. When all the chips are removed, go back and clean up any waste left in the V-grooves.

The 8 is another difficult character. Follow the two, continuous figure-eight shaped cuts indicated in the diagram and turn the workpiece gradually as you carve. The first cut begins at the top of the character.

The tightest curves are on the inside of the character. Remember to keep your knife tipped up a little to help you make it around those cuts with minimal chatter.

Be careful as you round the bottom of the character. Remember to decrease your depth of cut slightly as you approach the place where the line is parallel to the grain to prevent the knife from running with the grain.

There are many ways you can approach carving the 8. I like to cut each side of the continuous stroke in long, unbroken passes. Begin at the top of the character on the outside of the stroke. Follow that line back to where you began. You will cut on the outside of the stroke for the upper half of the 8, and on the inside for the lower half. Keep you knife angled up a little bit as you round the tighter curve—especially where the cut curves across the grain. You will rotate the workpiece almost constantly as you work.

Begin the second cut at the point where the figure-eight stroke intersects itself. Cut across the intersecting section and around the inside curve of the upper half of the figure. Again, keep your knife tipped up on tight curves. Follow the line until you return to where you began. Finish by removing waste in the groove.

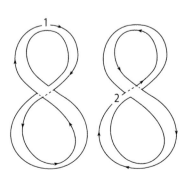

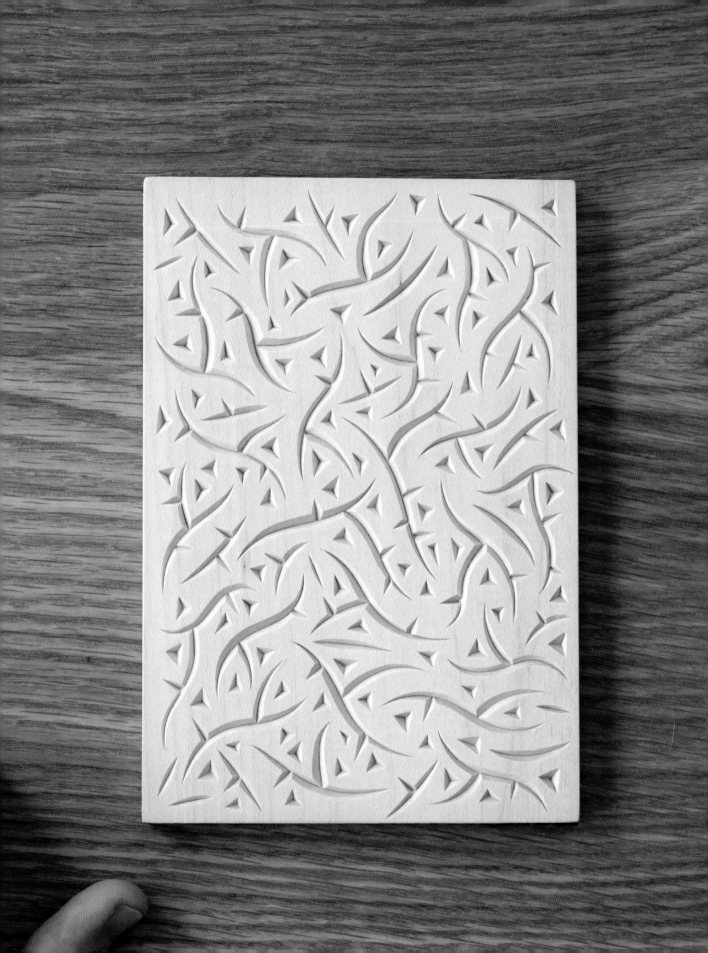

6 FREEHAND CARVING

In this chapter we venture as far afield from the common approach to chip carving as any book on the subject ever has, to my knowledge. My goal with this chapter is to drive you toward thinking of carving as an act of mark-making, and the knife as a mark-making tool, not so different from a piece of charcoal, or a brush loaded with ink or paint.

GUIDED FREEHAND CARVING

If you find the prospect of carving without a pattern intimidating, a few lines on an otherwise blank board will serve as visual references, easing you into the practice of letting your eyes guide the knife. Guided freehand carving is an intermediary step between carving on blank wood purely by eye, and carving to a pattern in which every single chip shape is delineated. Even if you relish the idea of abandoning patterns altogether, guided carving will only improve your skill at directing the knife with your eyes.

Guided freehand carving will also play a role in the chapter on creating "traditional" chip carvings, so this is a good opportunity to get some low-risk practice in on a piece of scrap or the back of one of your practice boards.

BASELINE GUIDES: THREE-CORNER CHIPS

Start by making some horizontal lines across the width of a board. Make sure the grain is running vertically, just like the grain orientation of the practice boards. These lines will serve as baselines for all of the three-corner chips you carve in this exercise. Everything above the baseline— the vertical height of each chip, the angles at which you cut—will be executed by eye.

Draw some lines across the grain of a piece of scrap. These lines will serve as a baseline for carving triangular chips by eye.

This should be a familiar sequence by now: First cut, First Position. Second cut, Second Position. Third cut, back to First Position.

Batch cutting works for free and semi-freehand carving as well. Space the chips as evenly as you can, but don't overthink it.

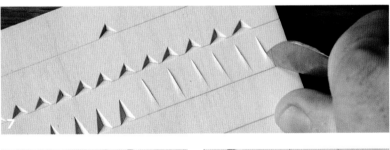

Try a variety of sizes and shapes of three-cornered chips. If needed, reference the practice board chapter for useful order-of-cut sequences.

How many lines and how far apart they are is up to you, but I recommend leaving enough space between them to carve a variety of small to medium chips. In the photo I am using my little metal ruler as a spacer to layout the lines, giving me about ⅝" between each line.

Start by carving a simple three-corner chip, approximately the size of the chips in the first few rows of Practice Board #1. Follow the same sequence of steps:

First cut in First Position, plunging until the edge of the blade reaches the baseline.

Rotate the board and make another plunge cut down to the baseline in Second Position.

Finally, relieve the chip from the board by cutting across the baseline in First Position.

Carve as many small chips as you like. If your chips aren't exactly the same size and shape as the three-corner chips in the practice board, don't worry about it. The goal is not to reproduce the printed chips with perfect accuracy, but to execute the same sequence of steps without a complete pattern to guide you.

Next, try batch cutting a series of the same size three-corner chip.

Now try a few larger chips. Notice that I'm carving these all in First Position.

GUIDED FREEHAND CARVING (CONTINUED)

Moving on, try carving some even larger three-corner chips. Just as with any other larger chip, you may find it necessary to remove them in stages: first remove the top half of the chip, then remove the waste at the bottom of the chip pocket by repeating your cuts.

For an added challenge, use a circle as the baseline. Because the circular baseline is constantly changing in relation to the direction of the grain, you will find that you need to alter the order of cuts for some of the chips.

CENTERLINE AND BASELINE GUIDES: TWO-CORNER CHIPS

For this guided freehand carving exercise, draw some more lines across the width of a board, diagonally this time. All the cuts in this exercise will be made in First Position, pulling the knife through the cut. The easiest orientation for this exercise is with the lines running diagonally across the grain from top left to bottom right—meaning that all of your cuts will be made with the grain. If you carve with your left hand, reverse this.

Start off with the tip of the knife on a line, and make a gently sweeping pull-cut away from and then back to the line. Now rotate the board 180° and make

Removing larger chips works the same way as with a printed pattern: Remove the chip in stages.

Try using a curved baseline and space the chips as evenly as you can by eye.

For the next exercises draw diagonal lines across a scrap board. Use the lines as centerlines or baselines for two-cornered chips.

In this exercise all of your cuts will begin and end with the tip of the knife on the line.

Just as with the three-cornered chips in the previous exercise, try carving a variety of sizes and shapes of two-cornered chips.

For two-cornered chips with one straight side and one curved side, the guidelines serve as baselines.

an identical cut (or as close as possible) to relieve the chip.

Don't be discouraged if you don't get a chip to pop out on the first try! Learning to gauge the depth of a given cut is one of the challenges of patternless carving. You might be wondering "But if I don't know how big the chip is going to be, how do I know how deep to cut?" Excellent question. You may find my answer unsatisfying, but it's the simple truth: it comes with practice and experience.

Don't be afraid to make a mess of a few chips. Your results are always telling you something about the way you're carving and the ugly, ragged messes you make are among the most instructive. Pay attention to them, and try again.

Carve a few more in the same manner, but try varying the length and width. Now try some with one straight cut that runs along the line and a curved relief cut.

GUIDED FREEHAND CARVING (CONTINUED)

Don't worry if your S-curves aren't perfectly symmetrical, or even if your lines aren't smooth and flowing. The point of this exercise is to internalize the feeling of carving curves. The lines give you a place to begin, a general direction, and a spot to aim for at the end of each cut.

There are two common tendencies when first beginning to carve freehand: carving too deep and carving with an angle of cut that is too high. The first of these will make for laborious carving— you are probably using more muscle than is necessary, tensing up, and focusing all of that tension into the point of the blade. Make sure your knife is very sharp, then try to relax and let it do the work for you.

The second of the two tendencies—carving with a too-high angle of cut—is related to the first. Perhaps, in order to bear down (with too much force) your elbow goes up, and when that happens the angle of cut increases. Again, relax. Allow the knife to do the cutting, your hand to hold the knife properly, and your arm to pull your hand through the cut.

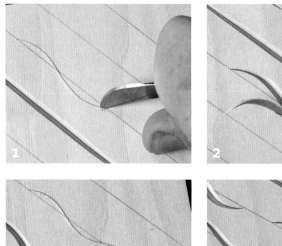

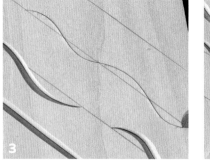
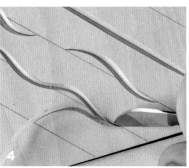

For wavy, serpentine two-cornered chips, don't think too hard about controlling exactly where the knife goes. Let motion of your arm create the shape of the curve.

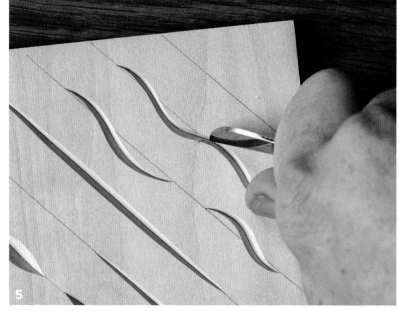

The improvisatory nature of freehand carving can make it difficult to gauge proper cut-depth, often resulting in the need to clean waste to out of the bottoms of chip pockets.

RADIAL DOODLES

Radial Doodles using two- and three-cornered chips.

These two exercises expand on the previous guided carving exercises. The goal here is not only to improvise the size and shape of each individual chip, but also to arrange them in a radial pattern as you carve. In short, I'm asking you to go a step beyond simply being a carver, and become a designer.

For this reason I urge you not to copy my radial doodle patterns chip for chip. Mimicking my choices in terms of specific chip shape, size and orientation would be beside the point. You will get much more out of this exercise if, instead, you make your own choices about what to put where, keeping in mind some general principles of ornamental radial pattern design: repetition, variation and symmetry. (I use the term "symmetry" loosely here, of course. After all, we are working largely by eye, and we are not machines.) I'll describe my thinking about the decisions I make along the way.

RADIAL DOODLES (CONTINUED)

PREPARING THE BOARDS

In the previous two exercises we used a series of parallel guidelines. For this exercise, divide a square board into eight equal segments by drawing four lines: two lines connecting the corners, and two lines connecting the midpoint of each side. This gives you eight line segments radiating from the center of the board. These are the only guidelines we'll use for this exercise.

RADIAL DOODLE #1

For my first radial doodle I've made the (entirely arbitrary) decision to use only S-shaped two corner chips. Feel free to choose a different approach.

I carve eight similar chips radiating from the center of the board, using the eight guidelines as centerlines for each chip.

Each pair of adjacent chips forms a negative space (which is to say an uncarved space) between them. My next decision is to carve similar chips in those blank spaces. This is where I begin to introduce some simple variation by reversing the direction of every other chip.

For this particular carving, I decided that those two "rules"— fill the spaces between adjacent chips with similar chips, and reverse the direction of every other chip—would be my decision-making framework for the rest of

For the Radial Doodle exercise draw lines radiating from the center of a board.

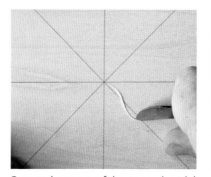
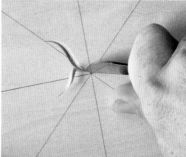

Start at the center of the crossed guidelines, working your way around and out from the center.

The guidelines will help you maintain a generally symmetrical layout, but don't fret too much about being "perfectly" symmetrical.

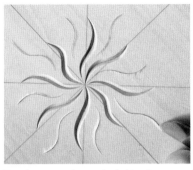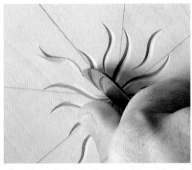

For the second round of chips I reverse the direction of the S-shaped chips. Simple variations like this will give your carving some motion and liveliness.

Temporarily reduce the depth of your cut when making a relief cut that changes direction relative to the grain.

Carve as many chips as you want. It's your doodle, and only you can say when it is time to stop carving.

the carving. In a very informal sense of the term, that framework is my "algorithm" for generating the overall design.

Remember as you carve that all the principles of good technique and paying attention to grain orientation also apply to freehand carving. One of the purposes of these exercises is to further internalize the good carving habits you developed in the first half of the book. They may never become fully unconscious (personally, I am always thinking about the quality of my technique to some degree) but they will begin to feel more natural, and less conscious.

In this photo, I am making a relief cut on a curvy chip that runs parallel to the grain. Remember to lift the knife a little as the cut changes direction in relation to the grain. This will prevent the cut from "running" along the grain.

As I continue to add chips, I frequently pause and look at the carving as a whole to decide what to add next and whether or not it feels complete. I can't tell you when your pattern is complete. That is a matter of personal taste. Stop when it feels right. Or, if you're not sure, set it aside and come back to it later. Revisiting it after a break often helps see it with new eyes.

RADIAL DOODLES (CONTINUED)

RADIAL DOODLE #2

For the second doodle I decide to use three-corner chips, starting with a small one on each of the eight guidelines.

This time I've decided to leave the center of the board empty and arrange my first chips in loose ring.

Similar to how I approached the previous radial doodle, my next decision is to fill in the space between my first eight chips. After filling the gaps with slightly longer, skinnier chips, I add another ring of chips on the eight guidelines.

Next, another round of small chips centered on the guidelines, followed by more in the spaces between. I space them as evenly as I can by eye. After adding this round of chips my pattern is starting to feel truly circular.

Start with a single chip. In this case I'm using the guidelines as centerlines for the first round of three-cornered chips.

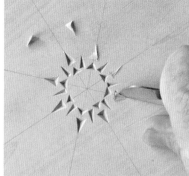

Working my way around and out from the center, I vary the size and shape of chips.

Repetition and variation are common techniques for giving a radial design a sense of rhythm. This ring of chips repeats the general size and shape of the first ring.

Batch cutting helps on two fronts: It makes spacing chips evenly easier and it moves things along at a quicker pace.

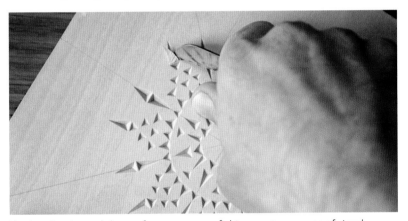

Varying the size and shape of some groups of chips creates a sense of visual "punctuation"

Notice the repetition: the border chips are roughly the same size and shape as the very first ring of chips I carved.

Continuing as before, I add more chips in the new blank spaces. Batch cutting will help you space things evenly and keep the size and shapes consistent.

As I work my way out from the center, the pattern grows, one ring of chips at a time. The guidelines help me keep things (more or less) evenly spaced and radially symmetrical. Notice how the simple variation of which way my triangular chips are pointed creates a sense of mild visual tension—some chips are pointed out toward the edges, while some point in toward the center.

After a few more groups of chips I decide that my design is getting close to being complete, but I want to emphasize that feeling of completeness. A common and effective way to do that with radial patterns is to add a border. I decide to compose my border of small three-corner chips.

RADIAL DOODLES (CONTINUED)

I like where it's heading, but it's not quite there yet. Adding another round of small chips pointed in the opposite direction creates a loose zig-zag effect and makes for a much bolder, more effective boarder. From a conceptual standpoint, I also like that the border echoes the tension in the rest of the pattern—some chips pointed out, some pointed in.

But it still doesn't feel quite complete to me, so I add one final ring of chips, a final border around the zig-zag border. To my eye, this resolves the in/out tension once and for all and feels complete. "Out" wins.

Is it perfectly symmetrical and circular? No! Is that okay? Yes! I enjoy the undulating irregularity of freehand carvings. Some of my favorite chip carvings are folk carvings from around the world that were, by all appearances, executed largely by eye and exhibit wild irregularities, asymmetries, and surprising variations.

The second group of border chips faces the opposite direction. This adds to the visual "weight" of the border and creates a little in-versus-out tension.

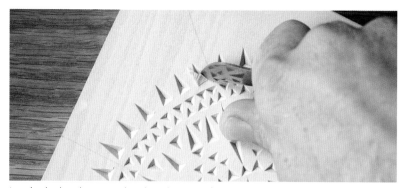

Lastly, the border gets a border. This ring of larger chips give the design a final sense of "pop!" that I like.

With the final ring of large three-cornered chips radiating from the border, this doodle is complete.

SYMMETRICAL TOWERS

The Symmetrical Towers exercise requires you to combine your technical and visual skills with your imagination and creativity. The result is that all improve.

To get started, draw one or more evenly spaced, parallel lines on a board. Draw another along one edge to serves as a baseline.

Build your towers up from the bottom, and out from the centerlines

The next exercise in guided freehand carving is simple to explain, but quite challenging. Here's how it works.

Draw one or more lines on a blank board, either with or across the grain.

The lines represent the vertical centerlines of imaginary towers (or castles, shrines, pillars or monuments.) Add a baseline if you want—that can really help to get things off to a good start.

Begin building your towers, as all towers must be built: from the bottom up. The components of your tower can be any shapes you want, but you must build the tower symmetrically from the centerlines out. Keep things as neat, clean and symmetrical as you can.

You can see that for this set of three towers I am using intersecting chips. I carved the larger chips that cross the grain first, then carve a series of lines across them.

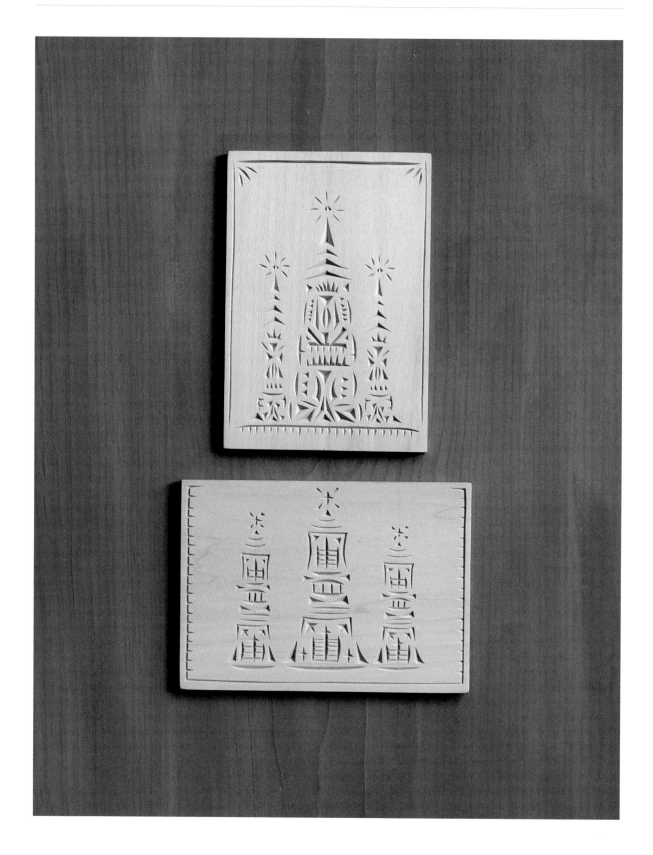

SYMMETRICAL TOWERS (CONTINUED)

In this example, I'm carving three towers on a single board, the center tower being the largest. As with the Radial Doodles, I am employing both repetition and variation to create a cohesive design. This is a useful design technique, especially if you are improvising a composition and don't know what to do next: Take an arbitrary decision that you already made—some shape or collection of shapes—and repeat it, but vary it in some way. The little grids of intersecting chips in these three towers are an example of this. I finish off the towers with some little star finials. Each star is composed of a small two-corner chip and a notch on each side.

The only thing that limits you here is your imagination, but sometimes even the most active imaginations get sluggish or exhausted. If you feel stuck, put it down and come back to it later. Or put the carving away long enough to clean your workspace and sharpen your knife. Taking a little breather can go a long way toward reseting your creative mind. And if you really don't want to stop carving, try simply switching gears for a bit: put away the exercise and pick up something with a printed pattern like a practice board and just carve some chips. Sometimes a little mindless repetition is all it takes to jog your brain into a creative mode.

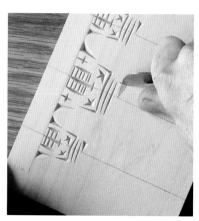

I wanted these towers to be similar to one another, so I built them as a group, instead of one at a time.

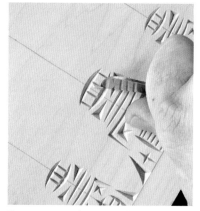

Try using a combination of two- and three-cornered chips, and intersecting or compound chip shapes. Think of this exercise as "drawing" with the knife.

Your towers don't necessarily have to follow the logic of real-life structures; they can be as wild and crazy as you want.

ECLIPSE

The board I carved my eclipse on was first painted with a blue-gray milk paint.

For laying out work on dark painted wood I use a white colored pencil instead of a standard graphite pencil.

In this project we will use a common principle of 2D image composition to create a simple stylized solar eclipse. As a carving exercise, the focus of this project is not so much about guiding the knife with your eyes, but rather treating the knife as an artist would pen and ink: sketch the basic design in pencil, then ink in the lines. Or in our case, carve them.

You can use any size "canvas" you like. Mine is fairly large, at roughly 12" x 18" (a 2:3 aspect ratio, proportionally speaking). I have also painted my board with milk paint.

Carving painted wood is very satisfying. Every mark you make stands out in stark relief against the painted "background," amplifying the feeling that carving is a kind of mark-making.

With milk paint I typically use two coats. Allow the first coat to dry thoroughly, then give it a very light sanding, and wipe off the chalky paint dust before painting on the second coat. After the second coat dries, another light sanding and wipe off the dust.

For laying out this project you will need a pencil, a long straightedge, and a compass. I'm using a white colored pencil so that my guidelines will stand out against the painted surface.

ECLIPSE (CONTINUED)

THE RULE OF THIRDS

To compose the eclipse image we'll use a well-known design principle called the Rule Of Thirds. If you have ever taken a photography class you are probably already familiar with the concept. It's an effective way of composing a dynamic image.

It's very simple, here's how it works: Divide the board, into thirds vertically and horizontally, and place subjects or points of interest at the intersections. I begin by finding the point where the left-most vertical line and the uppermost horizontal line intersect. We only need the point of intersection, so to avoid unnecessary erasing, don't draw lines all the way across the board.

Mark the point of intersection with a cross-hair.

Use a long ruler and the Rule of Thirds to locate the center point for the sun. Don't like the placement? Put yours wherever you like—it's your eclipse!

Make a temporary cross-mark for the sun's center. Colored pencil will erase easily enough, but use a sharp pencil and draw lightly.

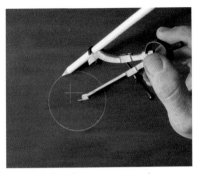

Draw a full circle to represent the moon's shadow. Offset it a little from the cross-mark.

Draw a semi-circle to represent the sun.

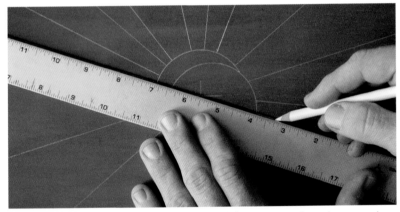

Lines radiating from the cross-mark represent light emanating from the sun and from behind the shadow of the moon.

The eclipse scene is taking shape now. There's no need to draw all the rays at this stage—you can always add more later.

Now draw a circle with the compass. Offset it bit from the cross-hairs, a little down and to the right. This will be our "shadow."

The size of the circle and how much you offset it is up to you. You can size and space things however you want, but think about the overall size of your image (determined by the size of the board you are working on) when making a decision. Also: don't over think it. Do what feels right.

Next, using the same compass setting, place the point of the compass directly on the cross-hairs and draw an arc that intersects with the shadow circle. This is our "sun."

Next, start laying out the lines that represent rays of light emanating from the partially eclipsed sun. All of these lines pass through the cross-hairs and extend to edge of the board.

Draw as many as you like—you can always erase or draw new ones later. Again, don't think about it too hard. Space your lines by eye and put them wherever it feels right to you.

ECLIPSE (CONTINUED)

BEGIN CARVING

Carve the line where the sun and the shadow of the moon meet. This is the only outline we'll carve. The rest of the sun and shadow shapes will be defined by where the rays terminate.

I start by carving the rays that define the shape of the sun, using the pencil lines as guides.

After carving chips along each of the guidelines radiating from the sun, I fill in the gaps with more. The lengths these chips are improvised, with a lot of variation from chip to chip, to give a sense of randomness.

Next I move on to the rays emanating from "behind" the moon shadow. I carve longer, skinnier chips for these rays, leaving the gaps between them blank. This helps create the impression that the light is partially blocked by the shadow.

Next I move on to carving the rays of light around the sun and shadow. For most of these I use the guidelines, the placement of some of them are made by eye.

Carve the line that represents the shadow overlapping the sun

The light rays that radiate from the sun and shadow can be batch carved.

The rays that emanate from "behind" the shadow are differentiated from the ones that come from the sun by shape; shorter more triangular chips for the sun, long tapering lines for the shadow.

After carving the rays emanating immediately from the sun and shadow, use the pencil lines as guides to begin filling in the surrounding rays.

Pencil in more rays to taste. All of the lines representing rays pass through the temporary cross-marks.

For rays that run off the edge of the board, stop a little before you get to the edge and tilt the knife down to finish out the cut.

Draw additional guidelines if you need to.

Be very careful carving lines that extend off the edge of the board. To prevent the knife from slipping out of the cut and onto your table (or worse, your lap) stop before you reach the edge, then complete the cut by rocking your knife downward to sever the remaining fibers.

I have only ever given my self a serious cut from chip carving once (yes, just once) and it happened while carving near the edge of a panel. The cut was directed toward the edge of the panel, and I simply forgot to stop the cut before I approached the edge. The knife slipped right through the last eighth of an inch or so of wood at the edge and zipped across my leg, through the canvas work pants I was wearing, the thermal long-johns beneath them, and then my thigh. Luckily it was not a deep cut, and because I keep my knives extremely sharp it healed very quickly. It was, however, a lesson I'll never forget. The lesson isn't really about chip carving but about remaining focused and aware of what your body is doing, where your body is in relation to the work you're doing, and the physics of the tools you're employing to do the work. In short, be careful, and most importantly: pay attention.

ECLIPSE (CONTINUED)

For cuts that begin at the edge of a board, your knife should look something like this, with the blade's edge pressed into the edge of the board. Don't use too much force here, you probably need less than you think.

Here you can see the V-shape formed by two opposing cuts.

FINISHING TOUCHES

This is another instance where I can't tell you when to stop carving. You have to decide for yourself when your carving is complete. When you are finished, erase whatever pencil lines remain.

I finished up my carving with another wash of milk paint, applied heavily over the entire board and immediately wiped off, to color in all of my carved lines.

To begin carving at the edge of the board hang the knife off the edge just a bit and pull through the cut as you normally would.

Pause periodically to asses the overall design and decide if you need to carve more rays.

To color in the lines, flood on the paint and then immediately wipe it off. Have plenty of paper towels or rags ready to go.

CHANGING ANGLES

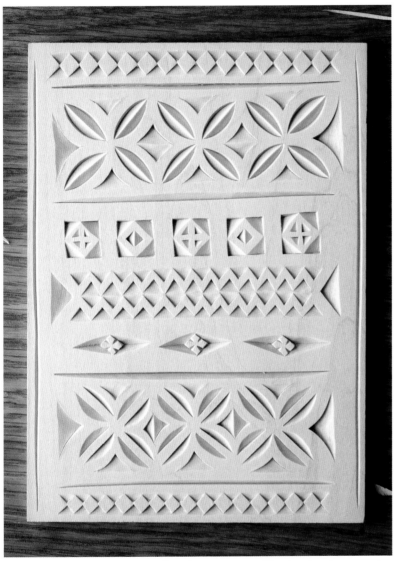

An improvised style board of motifs and patterns carved freehand and using a mix of high and low cutting angles.

Freehand carving provides a good opportunity to experiment with one of the most fundamental elements of chip carving technique: angle of cut.

Up to this point, we have been using a single angle of cut, somewhere between 45°-65° degrees (with the exception of instances where it is beneficial to alter the angle of the knife in mid-cut to prevent excessive undercutting of surrounding wood fibers.) Moreover, if you've read any of the popular how-to books on chip carving from the last few decades, you've likely run across instructions to develop and maintain a single, consistent angle of cut.

I think this is a good idea for first time chip carvers, up to a point. The most important goal when you are just starting out is to develop reliable control over the knife, and there is no better way to do that than through repetitive practice using a single angle of cut. If you have been working through this book chapter by chapter from the beginning, you have probably committed the feeling of carving at that primary angle to muscle memory. That's a good thing— the primary angle of cut is your technical home base.

However, a quick glance at the historical record of chip carving reveals how much stylistic variation is available to you simply

CHANGING ANGLES (CONTINUED)

by learning to vary the angle of cut. You see varied-angle chip carving all over the world—take some time to look at folk chip carvings (Google it!) from Russia, Sweden, Romania and the South Pacific Islands.

With a little experimentation and practice, you can significantly broaden your vocabulary of chip shapes and alter the visual impact of familiar shapes and patterns.

Speaking of familiar shapes, let's start with a small triangle. The first two cuts are made by plunging the knife into the wood at a very high angle, nearly 90° to the surface of the board.

The relief cut is made at an extremely low angle.

The result is a chip pocket with only a single visible wall (when

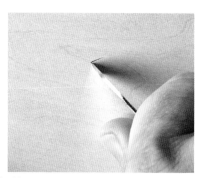

The first two cuts are made with the knife held at an almost-90° angle to the surface of the wood.

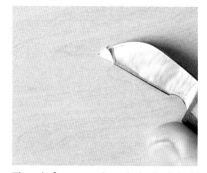

The relief cut is made with the knife held at a very low angle.

GRIP FOR LOW-ANGLE RELIEF CUTS

To establish a grip for making low-angle relief cuts, place the knife flat in front of you. Grasp it where it lies, with your index finger extended. Extending your index finger gets it out of the way, allowing you to make cuts at a very low angle.

Batch cutting mixed-angle chips. High-angle cuts first followed by the low angle relief cuts.

Extending the index finger allows you to lower the cutting angle of the knife.

The first row of chips serves as a guide for adding additional rows. A wide variety of border and grid patterns can be created working this way.

looking at the board straight on) that slopes down and seems to disappear beneath the two high-angle chip pocket walls.

Let's look at that again from a different vantage point, and also how to establish knife grips that will give you the necessary cutting angles.

The first two high-angle cuts are made using what is essentially a First Position grip, but with the knife held perpendicular (or almost perpendicular) to the wood. Notice that my thumb is still planted on the work piece, just like a standard First Position grip.

Give the varied angle grips a try and batch cut a row of small triangular chips like the one I started off with.

Add a few more rows of the same kind of chip and it's easy to imagine the kinds of borders and grids you can create with this style of carving. If you need some inspiration, pay special attention to carvings from the South Pacific and Romania.

CHANGING ANGLES (CONTINUED)

For this larger triangular chip, I've made two high-angle cuts (drawing the knife this time instead of plunging) and I am relieving the chip with a series of low-angle slices, starting at the tip of the triangle and shaving my way back to the baseline. Be gentle—it's easy to blow out the side walls of the chip pocket.

The four chips that make up this square motif should now look familiar: four varied-angle chips arranged at right angles (or as close as possible since we're working by eye.) Don't forget to employ batch cutting where you can. It will help you stay consistent and keep things moving along.

Two possibilities for center motifs.

For this motif I made four high-angle cuts to define the central diamond shape, followed by a primary angle cut (not an extra-low cut this time) from the corner of the diamond out, and another back toward the diamond. If the chip doesn't pop free, repeat your cuts until it does.

I finished these off with notch cuts, transforming the diamond into a flower. Again, this probably looks familiar.

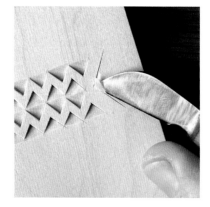
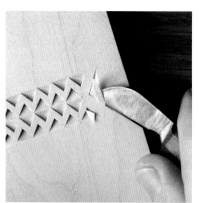

For larger mixed-angle chips, the high-angle cuts are pull cuts, and the chip is relieved gradually with a series of low-angle slicing cuts.

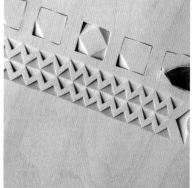

Four mixed-angle cuts are arranged to form diamond-in-a-square motifs.

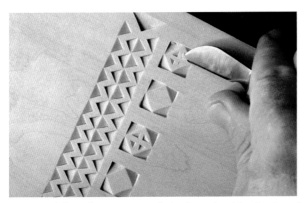

Two possibilities for center motifs, both made with mixed-angle triangular chips.

This motif is reminescent of the final row of Practice Board 2.

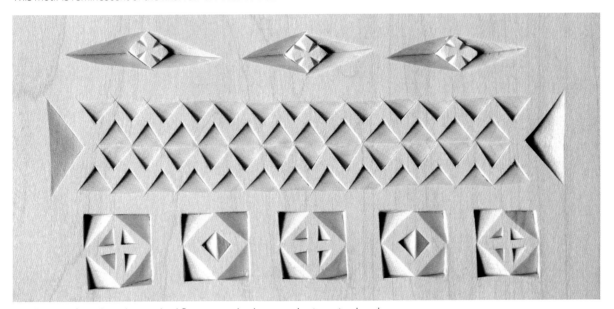

Familiar motifs such as the notched flower can also be carved using mixed angles.

CHANGING ANGLES (CONTINUED)

The varied-angle approach can also be applied to lines and long two-corner chips.

Remove leftover waste clinging to the bottom of the chip pocket as you normally wood, by repeating your cuts.

Here I am batch cutting the first two high-angle cuts of a series of petal-shaped motifs, trying to make my curved cuts as smooth as possible. It's okay if they are a little wonky.

Learning a new technique or concept often has the effect of making your eye keenly aware of it. Now that you have spent some time practicing carving chips with a mix of high- and low-angle cuts, I suggest searching out images and examples of chip carving around the world, especially work from previous eras. (Museum and art auction websites tend to be excellent sources of images of very old carving work from both professional artisans and folk artists.) I predict that you will immediately begin noticing just how common this technique is in the global historical record of wooden surface carving.

For mixed angle lines and two-cornered chips, make a high-angle pulling cut followed by a low-angle relief cut.

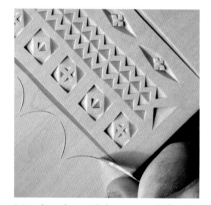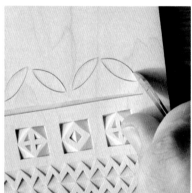

Mixed-angle petal shapes are defined with high-angle pulling cuts.

Relieve the two chips that form the petal shapes with low-angle relief cuts along a shared centerline.

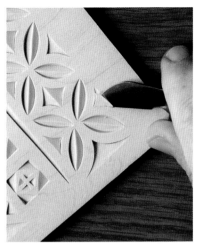

The spaces between petal shapes are filled in with curved mixed-angle triangular chips. Two curved, high-angle pull cuts define the shapes and the chips are removed with low angle cuts.

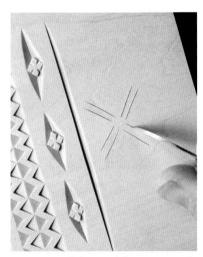

A variation of the petal shape is carved with straight high-angle pull cuts and curved low-angle relief cuts.

Next I relieve the center of the petals with two low-angle cuts, leaving a ridge along the middle of each petal.

After adding another row of petals mirroring the first, I add some large curvy triangles, making two high-angle cuts and then carving back to my imaginary baseline, bit by bit.

I add more curvy triangles in the available spaces to fill out the pattern. Remember, this was entirely improvised. It was not planned out or practiced ahead of time. And honestly, it shows: if you look closely at any one shape, the lines are a little wonky and the shapes are irregularly spaced, but it still works. Your eye sees the pattern, not the irregularities.

Next, I decide to try a variation on the petal shape.

I finish up my varied-angle practice board with a border at the top and bottom made of simple triangular chips arranged to form a row of diamonds.

DRAWING WITH THE KNIFE

The first example of freehand carving is a pattern I call the "Briar Patch," because of its vague resemblance to a thicket of thorny branches. I have included it to serve as a demonstration more so than a step-by-step project, but feel free to treat it as such. This is just a single iteration of the Briar Patch—it's different every time I carve it because I am improvising the shape, size and placement of the chips as I go. Follow my process in the photographs and try something like it yourself, or if the prospect of carving blank wood seems daunting to you, move on to the other exercises and projects in this chapter and come back to it.

Freehand carving, or carving without a printed or drawn pattern to follow, establishes a positive feedback loop between your intention and your muscle memory.

A chip shape originates in your mind's eye and is translated directly to the wood by your hand. The results tell you a number of things, but most importantly: whether or not you are using good carving technique and how well you are reading the grain.

The nice thing about freehand carving is that you can simply sit down and begin carving.

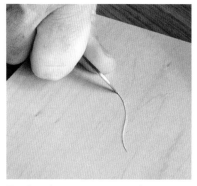
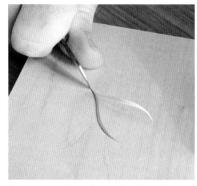

Freehand carving requires reliance on muscle memory. If you have developed good technical carving habits you can let your body handle the technical stuff and focus on the what marks to make where.

The Briar Patch "pattern" is really more of a texture. The first step is to indiscriminately cover the board with S-shaped marks.

Next, I add more S-shapes and curves, most of them intersecting with the first round of shapes.

Next come the thorns —these are notch cuts added to the tangle of intersecting serpentine marks.

The last step is to fill in the interstitial spaces with three cornered chips. My goal is for the pattern to completely fill the board with an even visual density marks.

To experience this directly, pick a shape, or a few shapes, and carve them over and over without a pattern to fall back on. Mix it up and experiment. Feel free to make a mess of a nice clean piece of basswood.

It doesn't really matter what you carve—developing a sense of artistic composition and design is not necessarily the primary goal, but it is one of the probably outcomes.

As you carve, pay attention to yourself telling your muscles what to do, and then observe the results. If something doesn't work, try to figure out what went wrong. The answer usually has to do with how you were holding the knife (technique) or how you ordered your cuts (grain.)

The inevitable outcome of practicing this way is that your technique and your reading of the grain will improve, and carving will feel more and more like a second-nature activity.

7 | TRADITIONAL CHIP CARVING

In this chapter we explore a way of working that integrates carving and design into a single practice. The projects documented here are not necessarily meant for you to copy or carve by rote. For the beginning and experienced carver alike, there are indeed technical lessons to be learned from the execution of these specific designs, but a deeper lesson will be learned by attempting the process itself: carving as you design, and *designing by carving.*

Throughout the chapter I use the daisy wheel—an ancient, common decorative form—to demonstrate a semi-improvisational approach to chip carving design. The daisy wheel outline and other simple forms are used as templates, to be fleshed out as the carver sees fit using a vocabulary of simple shapes and motifs. This is done either with minimal layout, entirely by eye, or with some combination of the two. As for the vocabulary of simple shapes, you know them already. They are the most recognizable hallmarks of chip carving, and for most of us they were among the first chip shapes we learned to carve: two- and three-cornered chips, and carved lines of various widths.

This workflow (to use a modern term) has been largely, if not entirely, neglected in chip carving how-to literature, yet evidence of it abounds in carvings from many places, periods, and stylistic traditions, up to the present day. You will see it in chip carved mangle boards from Northern Europe, ceremonial canoe paddles from the South Pacific Island nations, the elaborate ceremonial distaffs of Romania, wooden vessels and boxes from the Democratic Republic of Congo, and the Coptic Christian icon boxes of Ethiopia.

This is one of many ways to carve the traditional six-petal rosette, or "daisy wheel."

Design as you carve. The projects in this chapter are examples of how making decisions as you go leads to the final design.

There is an overall symmetry of content in this piece which your eyes likely read as "symmetrical," but look close at corresponding shapes and lines from one side of the board to the other and you will begin to see the asymmetries. Far from feeling incorrect, the tension created by regular overall patterning and irregular shapes creates a sense of liveliness.

Dig into the historical record of "vernacular" carvings form around the world and you will see daisy wheels everywhere and in every imaginable configuration.

Though the styles and uses of chip carving from these far-flung places and styles may differ, they share a similar spirit and aesthetic qualities: a loose and lively sensibility. The use of common forms (such as the daisy wheel) as templates allow for individualistic expression. The pleasing tension created by rendering regular, symmetrical geometries with the irregularity that is natural to working by eye. This is, in a deep sense of the term, traditional chip carving.

Some people may associate the daisy wheel symbol primarily with European decorative traditions or folkways. This is not entirely wrong, but it's not quite accurate, either. At the very least, it is only a small part of the picture. Use of the six-petal rosette (and its countless variations) stretches back to at least the Late Bronze Age where it appears on hammered golden discs from Mycanae (now southern Greece). It can be found carved in the limestone of Jewish ossuaries from first century Jerusalem, and was a common ornamental device in ancient Rome. Once again, the list is a long one. It is so old and so widely used that it can hardly be said to belong to any single place or time. It was traditional, in a manner of speaking, long before Europe, as such, existed.

The origin of the pattern is somewhat moot. My purpose is not to inflate the importance of a specific place, period, style or aesthetic sensibility, but instead to demonstrate that it is possible to use a simple shape as the seed for creative exploration. Each of the three projects in this chapter begin by drawing that same simple shape, yet they end up looking nothing alike. Moreover, from my perspective, the best possible outcome would be if your carvings end up looking nothing like mine. Yes, you read that correctly.

To get the most out of these projects, I suggest you commit yourself to deviating from my examples, at least a little bit here and there. As I will show you along the way, I make design decisions as I go, based on my personal tastes, inspiration from the carvings of previous ages, and a love of experimentation. There is no reason my decisions need to be your decisions. Nothing would make me happier than for you to choose your own adventure, so to speak.

This panel contains common historical ways of rendering the various parts of the daisy wheel rosette. Several will be instantly recognizable from the projects in this chapter and elsewhere in the book. It is not intended as an exhaustive stylistic glossary, but as inspiration for designing and styling your own rosette carvings.

MINI MANGLE BOARD 1

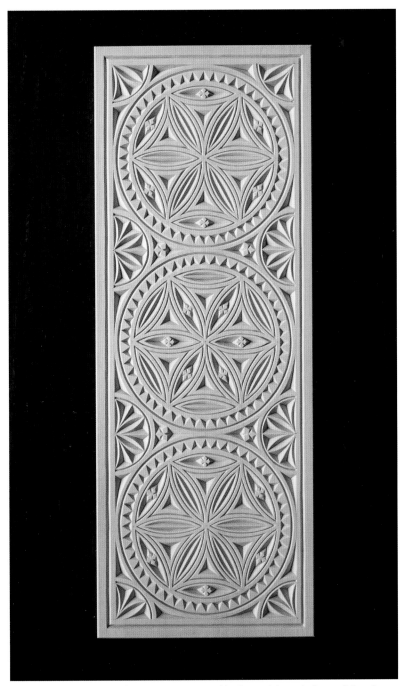

The small panels in this chapter were inspired by "mangleboards," a traditional tool used to press clothes and linens which became a poplar betrothal gift across Europe between roughly 1600 - 1900. Mangleboards were typically heavily decorated with carvings, paintings, or both.

I don't draft the entire design before I start carving, but develop it as I go, making decisions about what to add one element at a time. Let me restate that to underscore how I am working through this project: I start out with a blank board and only a vague idea of what the final will look like. This is the first time I've ever carved this specific design. It was not drafted ahead of time. If I made different decisions along the way—or even started with a board of a different size—it might look very different in the end.

Though I didn't know exactly what I would end up with, I started with a few general constraints and goals in mind. These largely determined the general feeling and visual impact of the piece:

- Use rosettes, borders, and common design elements to fill up the board.
- The central element of the design will be three rosettes of equal size and spacing.
- Use similar elements in each rosette, but variation between center and flanking rosettes.
- Each rosette gets an identical border of simple triangular chips and a bold border line.

MINI MANGLE BOARD 1 (CONTINUED)

I began with a piece of basswood about 6" x 16." My layout tools include a long ruler or straightedge, dividers, compass, pencil and eraser, a tape measure, and a 6" rule. I use the rulers primarily as straightedges—specific dimensions and proportions were determined by eye, and using the dividers to divide lines into segments of equal length. Depending on how comfortable you are eyeballing things, you may decide not to measure anything at all. If that sounds crazy, just stay with me.

After drawing a centerline along the length of the board, I marked the center of that line and drew the first circle. The compass setting was determined by eye and experimentation. The goal was to fit three circles on the board, tangent to one another, but with space along the edges and ends of the board. These circles define the boundaries of the three rosettes, including their borders.

I used smaller compass settings to draw three circles inside the first three. This established the width of the rosette borders and the overall size of the rosettes. Once again, this compass setting was determined by eye. I wanted a border of simple triangular chips around each rosette, the chips not too big, not too small. I eyeballed a width that seemed somewhere in that Goldilocks zone.

Layout begins by marking a center line along the length of the board.

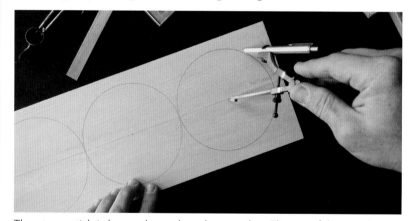

Three tangential circles are drawn along the centerline. The size of these circles was somewhat arbitrary, but ended up steering me toward certain other design decisions down the road. Being open to the results of experimentation is part of the joy of this process.

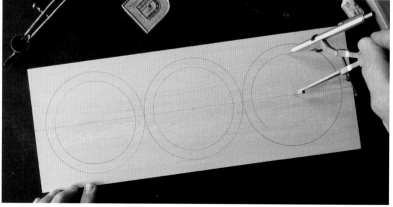

Smaller circles are drawn inside the first three circles. This creates three spaces for rosettes with borders.

LAYING OUT THE DAISY WHEEL

The basic daisy wheel form is drawn with a single compass setting. First, draw the perimeter circle and set the compass point somewhere on it. Draw an arc that intersects the perimeter in two places. The points where the arc intersects the perimeter become new locations for your compass point.

Draw five more arcs to complete the six center petals. To lay out the perimeter petals, place the compass on the outer end of each petal and strike temporary overlapping arc segments outside the daisy wheel to locate the necessary compass points.

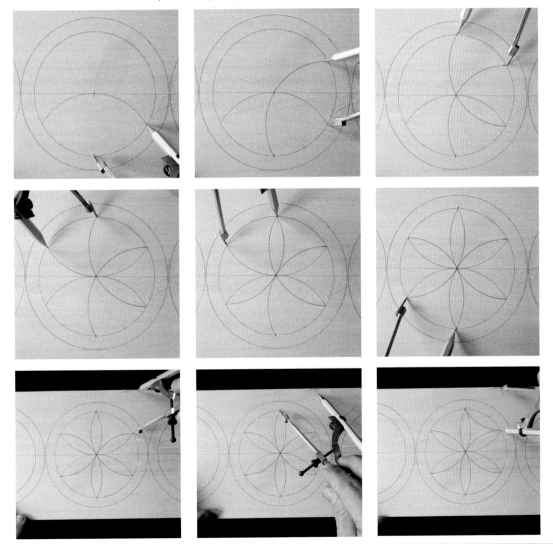

MINI MANGLE BOARD 1 (CONTINUED)

The first decision I made about how I would carve the daisy wheel rosettes was to leave the lines themselves uncarved and outline each individual shape within the rosette. Using the compass lines as a visual guide, I offset the carved outlines by about $^1/_{16}$" inside the lines of each drawn shape. Working in First Position, my first cuts are made with the knife facing the center of each shape to be outlined, followed by opposing cuts to relieve each outline. The outlines are about $^1/_{16}$"-thick. I followed this process for every shape in the daisy wheel.

I decided to treat the other two rosettes in the same manner, carving the outlines of each shape in the rosettes.

After the daisy wheel form is drawn in with pencil, the outlines of each shape are carved. For this mini mangle board I leave the lines uncarved and use them as visual guides.

Here's a daisy wheel with all of its shape outlines carved. Note that I left all the pencil marks in place and carved around them by eye.

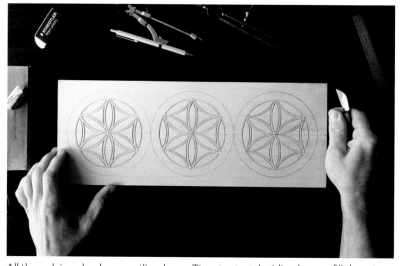

All three daisy wheels are outlined now. Time to start deciding how to fill them in.

It is entirely possible to proceed from this point without adding any more guidelines, but in this case I want to end up with fairly regular chip shapes and sizes so I pencil in some lines to help. I start by giving each of the six petals a centerline, then a cross line in the middle of each centerline.

I use dividers to help me create the points for a diamond in center of each petal.

Connecting the dots I located with the dividers to create the diamond shapes.

My next big decision about the design of the rosettes was to fill the central six petals of the center daisy wheel with a very common motif, the flower-in-petal motif.

To lay out the flower-in-petal motifs, I first draw centerlines through the six central petals and a line crossing each one. Using a straight edge, these lines are easily found by connecting the opposite points of each petal. The cross-lines can be found by connecting the points of the curvy triangular shapes on either side of a given petal.

Next, I use a pair of dividers to layout the points of the diamonds that are the basis for the Gothic flowers. I want the flower-in-petal motif to be a little smaller than my carved outlines, so I set the dividers a little narrower than the cross-lines. I mark the points by making very slight pricks in the wood with the dividers, placing them by eye, then connect the points with a straightedge. You could also sketch the diamonds in entirely by eye or carve without any lines at all.

MINI MANGLE BOARD 1 (CONTINUED)

Next I remove the compound chips around the diamonds. This should look familiar to you by now. If you need a refresher, look back at the last row of Practice Board 2 (pages 55-56).

One crucial difference, aside from size and proportion, between the pattern in Row 18 and these chips is that I am carving in part by eye, using the carved outlines as visual guides as I define the long sides of each compound chip.

Before we go any further let's take a moment to study the work so far—the carved outlines, and the diamond-in-petal motifs. All of it has been done in part by eye. So, naturally, there are little irregularities to be found everywhere, slight asymmetries and variations in line width. Now take another moment to meditate on this question: *Is that okay?*

I'm afraid I can't answer that question for you; I can only answer it for myself. I have no doubt that my carving would be more "perfect" if all of these shapes had been drawn out with exquisite geometric regularity, or designed in computer software and transferred to the wood. However, when I work in this design-by-carving mode, geometric perfection is not high on my list of priorities. I carve as carefully and as cleanly as I can. My eyes and my hands are not

The compound chips around the diamonds are removed first. This is the same process that is detailed in the Practice Boards chapter on pages 55-56.

All of the chips surrounding the diamonds have been removed in the center daisy wheel.

I pencil in more guidelines by giving each petal on the perimeter a centerline.

The first cut is made with the knife facing away from the center of the rosette.

The first cut of the second two-cornered chip is made away from the first two-cornered chip.

Finally, the second two-cornered chip is removed. This cut is offset from the carved outline by eye.

To move onto the border, I start by refining the border shape and size with a couple more compass lines.

perfect, and so neither will my work be geometrically perfect. Yet it *is* perfect in the sense that it is a perfect record of the eyes and hands that made it. These are *my* marks in the wood. How can I not love them?

I decide to give the six petal shapes around the perimeter of the rosette a much simpler treatment. I start by drawing a centerline through each petal. I do the rest of the work with the knife, once again using the existing outline as a visual guide to define the curved side of each long, two cornered chip.

Next, I decide to lay out and carve a border of simple triangular chips around the central rosette. My first step is to define the border with two additional circles. All of the chips that make up the border will live inside these two lines.

MINI MANGLE BOARD 1 (CONTINUED)

A simple way to divide the border is to use the a straightedge and the points of the central daisy wheel petals to mark out six equal divisions, then use the inner points of the curvy triangles to lay out six additional divisions. With the border divided into twelve equal segments, I use the dividers to divide each of those segments in half, making small tick marks with a pencil as I work my way around the border, for a total of twenty-four equal(-ish) divisions. I do one more round of divisions, eyeballing my tick marks this time, bringing the total to forty-eight segments.

The final step (or next to final step, depending on your level of comfort with semi-patternless carving) in laying out the triangular border is to mark the inner circle with tick marks *between the tick marks on the outer circle*. Once again, I'm doing this by eye.

To aid in spacing the triangular chips for the border I mark out divisions using the points of the shapes within the daisy wheel and a straightedge.

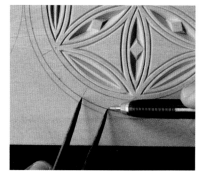

Next I use the dividers to divide the spaces in two again, from there the remaining divisions are marked by eye.

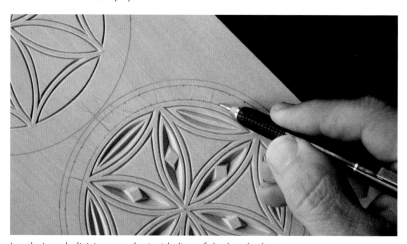

Lastly, I mark divisions on the inside line of the border by eye.

The sides of the triangular chips can be penciled in or you can simply connect the marks by eye with the knife itself.

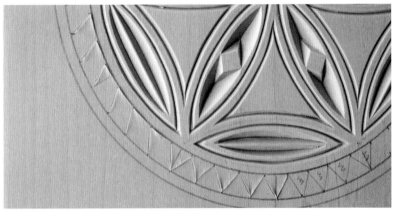

As the triangular chips change orientation to the grain, I change my order of cut so that my final cut will be crossing the grain.

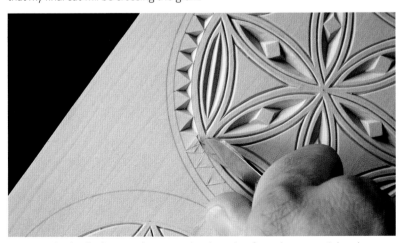

Here I make the final cut on the triangular chips that form the rosette's border.

At this point there are two ways to proceed. You can simply begin carving, using the tick marks on the outer circle as starting points, aiming your cuts at adjacent tick marks on the inner circle. Or, if you are hesitant to rely on your eyes to guide the knife, you can pencil in each line of the border chips before you carve them. Two lines for each chip of the forty-eight chips gives you ninety-six little lines, or ninety-six times you'll need to line up your straightedge, mark a line, and reset before you begin carving. You can probably guess which approach I would suggest, but it's up to you!

As I work my way around the border, the orientation of each chip changes relative to the direction of the grain. Accordingly, the most preferable order of cuts changes. In this photo, notice that there are two groupings of chips that differ based on which cuts I've made first, or rather, which cut I want to be last; all of the chips are now prepared for me to make a final, relief cut that crosses the grain.

MINI MANGLE BOARD 1 (CONTINUED)

My next decision is to outline the border with a relatively heavy (read: wide) carved line, but the existing boundary circle line looks a little too thick to me. I also want a little more space between each rosette, so I set my compass and redraw a slightly smaller circle.

To remove the thick border line, I start the first cut on the long grain side of the rosette, just a little bit above the point where the line is perfectly parallel to the grain, carving away from the center of the rosette, rotating the piece gradually as I cut. Likewise, the relief cut starts on the long grain side. Be careful on the long grain side of circular border lines like this. You can prevent the cut from "running" with the grain and thus outside of the line by lifting the knife out of the cut a little as you come around the point where the cut reverses direction relative to the grain. You can then return to that spot with a full depth cut to relieve it from the wood.

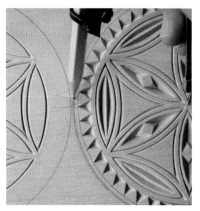
I leave a little space between the border of each rosette so can adjust by redrawing the outermost line.

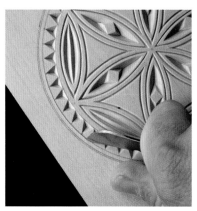
The first cut for the exterior borderline is made with the knife facing away from the center of the rosette.

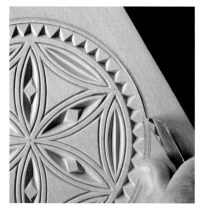

As you make the relief cut for the borderline, decrease the depth of cut as you reach the point where the line becomes parallel to the grain, then repeat the cut at that point to fully sever the fibers.

Sometimes it takes more than one additional cut to get the chip to release.

The last step in the center rosette is to fill in the curvy triangular spaces between the petals with large triangular chips. Instead of drawing each shape in full, I pencil in guidelines extending from the points of the curvy triangles toward the center.

The final design decision for the center rosette is how to treat the curvy triangular spaces formed by the petals. I've decided to fill them in with three-cornered chips, approximately twice as large as the chips that make up the border. A little layout helps me center them in their spaces. Using a straightedge lined up with the opposite points of any two adjacent curvy triangles, I pencil in three lines in each space. Those lines give me an indication of where to start and finish my cuts. The path of each cut is directed by my eye, following the curve of the surrounding lines.

These chips are a little on the large side, so I remove them in stages. The first three cuts define the shape of a chip and allow the top half to pop free of the board. Next I remove the remaining waste with additional passes at the same angle.

And there you have it: The first rosette is complete!

The cuts for the large-ish triangular chips are made by eye, but the guidelines provide an idea of where to start and stop.

MINI MANGLE BOARD 1 (CONTINUED)

From here I carved the flanking rosettes, using design elements and methods from the first rosette, but inverting the petal pattern—diamond-in-petal motifs on the six perimeter petals and six central petals filled with pairs of two-cornered chips. Now I can lay out the rest of the board.

My first decision is to draw one final circle around each rosette. I set the compass so that each circle is tangent with the carved border line of the neighboring rosettes. With this setting, the new circles form an overlapping band that bounds all three rosettes.

In the process of drawing these circles I discover a happy accident—the width of the band formed by these circles closely matches the width of the bands that separate the rosettes from their borders of triangular chips. I like the repetition, but it wasn't planned. Remember that I am developing this design as I go, making decisions on the fly, using common shapes and ornamental motifs to fill in the age-old daisy wheel forms. If I had placed the rosettes a little further apart, or made them smaller, this particular detail might have ended up being very different. Maybe this band would be wider, maybe I would have decided to do something entirely different.

Obviously, this exploratory, improvisatory process is not the

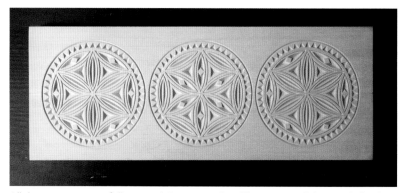

All three rosettes are fully carved. Reversing the "fill patterns" of the petals for the flanking rosettes creates some variation while maintaining a consistent style.

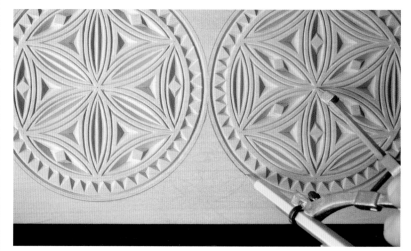

An additional circle around each rosette creates a conjoined band outlining all the rosettes.

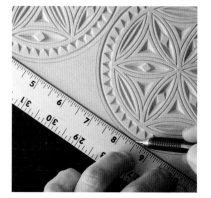

Drawing lines that are parallel to the edges of the board and tangent to the circles around the rosettes establishes the mini-mangle board's border and defines spaces between the rosettes and the border.

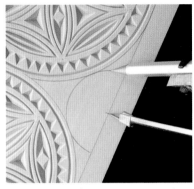
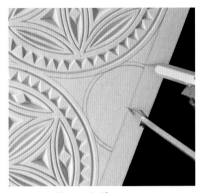

The the spaces between any two adjacent rosettes will get a half-rosette.

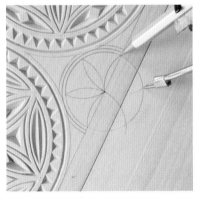

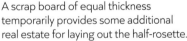

A scrap board of equal thickness temporarily provides some additional real estate for laying out the half-rosette.

Using a straight edge I add a few more details to the space between the rosettes.

The completed layout for the space between rosettes—as you'll see in the following steps I make a last minute decision that deviates from what I've drawn here.

only way to work, but if you're willing to set out with no idea of where you might end up, it is enjoyable. I love building a design one piece at a time.

Moving on with the current board, I lay out lines parallel to the edges and ends of the board. If I decide to add a border around the edge of the board, it will live between these lines and the edges of the board.

Next I turn my attention to the spaces formed by the rosettes and boundary lines. These spaces are handled in a variety of ways in folk and artisan carvings. Half-rosettes, fan motifs, leaves or floral motifs, heart shapes, grids of triangles or diamonds—all are common ways of filling in similar spaces. I decide to fill the spaces with half-rosettes. I start by marking the center of the space along the edge boundary, then mark a semi-circle tangent to the band surrounding the rosettes. I reset the compass wider and draw another semi-circle to create a band that intersects with the rosette band. One more semi-circle, this one with a smaller radius than the first, echoes the carved line that surrounds the border of triangular chips—this arc and the adjacent arc define it.

Using the same compass setting and point, I begin laying out the half-rosette. Butting a board of equal thickness up against the edge of my workpiece

MINI MANGLE BOARD 1 (CONTINUED)

allows me to easily lay out half of a daisy wheel. Then I fill in the triangular space between the central rosettes and the half rosette. I decided that a little triangular notched flower bud fit perfectly in that space and match the notched Gothic flowers in the rosettes. I pencil in three little tick marks, placing them by eye, and connect them with a straightedge.

The final layout step before I return to carving is to divide the spaces between the petals of the half-rosette. I also drew centerlines through each half-rosette petal, intending to mimic the petals containing pairs of long two-cornered chips in the central rosettes. As you will see, however, I later abandoned this idea and carved away each petal in full.

First, I remove the borderline around the half-rosette, then the half-petals, then work through the other shapes in the half-rosette.

After accessing the look of the first few two-cornered chips in the half-rosette, I decided to carve away the petals in full. My rationale was based only on intuition—I felt that carving the petals two-cornered chips would look busy and unbalanced. I then removed the three-cornered chips surrounding the half-rosettes and triangular flower buds.

For the corners I layout and carve quarter-rosettes—the

 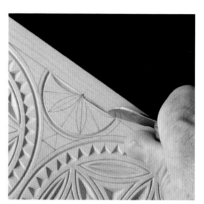

I start by removing the band around the half-rosette, followed by the half-petal shapes.

The petal chip being removed was drawn it as two separate two-cornered chips, but I changed my mind and carved a single full-petal shaped chip.

The three-cornered chips are removed last.

The corners get a similar treatment. Instead of a half-rosette, they are filled in with quarter-rosette.

The border line bounding the main design can be drawn with a combination square, or you can use the "finger trick."

The border lines are removed with long, opposing cuts.

Finally, I "ease" the edges of the board with a small block plane. If you don't have a block plane, use a piece of fresh sandpaper wrapped around a block of wood.

procedures are essentially the same as for the half-rosettes.

My final decision was to carve a simple border around the entire carving. You can lay out this line using a combination square registered on the board's edge. Or if you're feeling confident, try the "finger trick": Your hand takes the place of a square or marking gauge. Hold the pencil in a locked grip with the point on the surface of the wood and your middle finger against the board's edge. Drag your hand down the length of the board, keeping your hand locked and your finger registered as you draw.

After carving the border, I notch the diamond and triangular flower buds. For a finishing touch, I chamfer the board's edges using a block plane held at 45°. Chamfering the long grain edges of the board before you chamfer the ends helps prevent blowout. No plane? Chamfer the edges using sandpaper wrapped around a block of wood.

MINI MANGLE BOARD 2

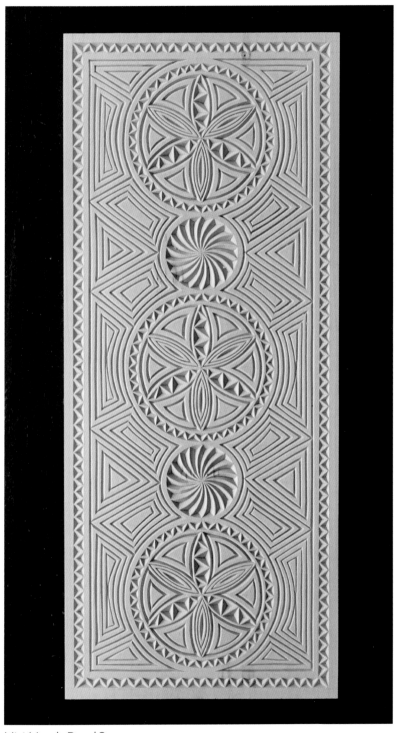

Mini-Mangle Board 2

I took a different stylistic approach with this mini mangle board, filling in the space around the rosettes with blocks of concentric shapes. The shapes were initially defined with pencil lines that served as visual guides for carving in each block of concentric shapes by eye. Take a close look at the degree of variation between the shapes on one side of the rosettes, and the corresponding shapes on the other side. There's a significant amount of variation, but it works as a whole, and the variation gives it a feeling of gently undulating movement. The pattern was inspired (not directly copied) by images of folk carvings from both Scandinavia and the South Pacific Islands.

The dimensions of the board are about 6.75" x 15.75". There's nothing special about those dimensions, and given that the goal of this chapter is to illustrate a workflow the relies on improvisation and working by eye, they aren't even particularly important. If I had chosen a board with different dimensions, that would likely have led to different design decisions, and resulted in a different finished carving.

MINI MANGLE BOARD 2 (CONTINUED)

My first step is to layout the daisy wheels. I drew a centerline along the length of the board, put one daisy wheel in the center, and the other two equally spaced from the ends of the board. Following my list of guidelines, I left plenty of space between the daisy wheels, did not draw in perimeter petals, and also left some space at each end of the board for the final border.

Because I had already decided that each rosette would have a border, I went ahead and drew two circles. The inner circle separates the border from the daisy wheel a little, the outer circle represents the outermost boundary of the border. The width of the border was determined was chosen somewhat arbitrarily. I might have changed my mind later, but I ended up sticking with it. I also went ahead and marked the border with six divisions along the axes of the petals. This is the only layout for the daisy wheel rosettes. From this point on I worked by eye.

Once again, I start the layout by first deciding on the placement of the rosettes.

In addition to the basic daisy wheel form, I draw two additional circles that define the border, plus some dividing marks that I will use later when carving the border pattern.

Mixed fill patterns within a single daisy wheel are a common trait of many vernacular chip carvings. Three petals get a zig-zag pattern, the other three are carved with two concentric petal-shaped lines and a single two-cornered chip in the middle.

I chose two patterns for the alternating petals. The first is a series of zig-zagging triangles. I started from the center, carving each triangle by eye and getting them as close to one another as I dared.

For the other pattern I chose to first outline the petal shape, and then fill in the center with concentric shapes. Here again I'm taking cues from my list of design guidelines—I've already decided that I want to use blocks of concentric shapes to fill in the spaces around the rosettes, so using the same theme here will tie the rosettes to the surrounding space thematically.

After carving the petals I outline the spaces between them with a bold, thick carved line. I have been carving primarily in First Position (I work in First Position as often as I can for the sake of consistency, and because I find it better for making long curving cuts) but in this scenario I switch to Second Position to facilitate carving in a specific direction—I want my cut to move in the opposite direction of the weak cross-grain point near the center of the rosette.

The spaces between petals are outlined with a heavy V-groove.

MINI MANGLE BOARD 2 (CONTINUED)

Here you can see that I have stopped my cut just short of completely relieving the chip, then turned the workpiece around to finish removing the piece with a small cut from the opposite direction. In some situations this is a good way to protect delicate cross-grain points.

Once the bold outlines are carved I repeat the shape in the remaining spaces. This is another nod to the theme of filling space with concentric shapes. To create some contrast between the petals and the spaces between them I keep the lines bold and only repeat the shape once. For the border I'll echo the zig-zagging triangles from the petals. I begin by carving three-cornered chips centered on the six division marks I made earlier, and then fill the spaces between with similar chips. These chips are sized and spaced by eye.

With the first row of border triangles carved, I start removing the outer row. This is a tricky operation—it's very easy to chip out the ridges between adjacent triangles if you cut too aggressively. If you have trouble with this border pattern, try making shallow scoring cuts first and then deepening them.

With the daisy wheel rosettes carved I turn my attention to the spaces between and decide to

The short-grain point at the corner of this shape is protected by stopping the relief cut short and finishing it up from the other direction.

I used the marks made earlier to carve in the first six triangular chips for the border pattern, then fill in the spaces by eye.

use another very common rosette design: spiral rosettes. You will find variations of spiral patterns in ornamental work of every kind, in every medium, throughout history and all over the world.

On the centerline that runs the length of the board, I locate the midpoint between adjacent daisy wheel rosettes and set my compass to draw a circle a little smaller than the given space. With the same compass setting I draw six arcs. Start by placing the point of the compass at an intersection of the circle and the centerline. Draw an arc from the circle's center to its edge. Now place the compass point at the intersection of the circle and the arc you just drew. Draw another arc as before. Repeat until you have six arcs radiating from the center of the circle.

The zig-zag border pattern echoes the zig-zag petal fill-pattern.

The spaces between the daisy wheel rosettes receive spiral rosettes. Like daisy wheels, spirals can be drawn with a single compass setting.

MINI MANGLE BOARD 2 (CONTINUED)

Divide one of the segments into thirds and mark the divisions (instead of marking the divisions with a pencil, I made very slight impressions with the dividers). Then repeat the process, starting from each of the new points in turn until the spiral is complete.

I carve the spiral rosettes one chip at a time, working my way around. Notice where I started—or rather where I will finish up. I want the last chip I carve to be one that is oriented generally parallel to the grain because the walls that separate it from its adjacent chips are stronger than chips whose walls cross the grain.

After I finish the spiral rosettes I mark a boundary around the edges and ends of the board to separate the main carving from the border. Then I began carving an outline around the rosettes with a series of long continuous cuts, offset from the rosettes by about ⅛" and using them as a visual guide for my cuts.

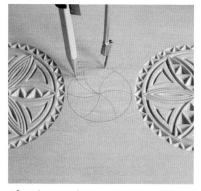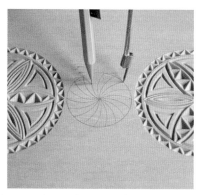

After drawing the outer circle and six evenly spaced arcs, the spaces between are divided by eye into three smaller spaces. Each dividing point becomes a compass point location and termination point for a new arc.

Carve the spiral rosette one chip at a time, always making the first cut for each new chip away from the previously carved chip.

There are two chips in the spiral that are oriented more or less in line with the grain—one of these chips should be your last chip in the rosette.

These lines are carved in by eye, offset from the rosettes about ⅛".

A second pass removes the long chips that define the space between the rosettes and the border. The width of these V-groove lines are determined by eye. In this case my lines are about ⅛" wide.

Design is just another way of saying "making some decisions." There are any number of ways I could have divided this space into smaller shapes. I decided to use the center of the spiral rosettes and the tips of the petals as starting/ termination points for my lines.

 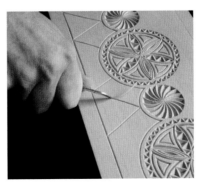

A second pass for each line removes the V-groove chips. I tried to match the line width used for outlining the larger space.

I joined this outline to the rectangular boundary line to create a large, irregular field of negative space bound by a thick outline.

To define the blocks of space to be filled with concentric outlines, I pick what I considered to be "strong" points in the assembly of rosettes—the points of the daisy wheel petals and the center point of each spiral rosette—and carve lines radiating from those points and intersecting at the edge boundary. These lines will intersect with the border that defines the large irregular field and divide it into a field of triangles and irregular trapezoids.

This is one of those places where your design decisions might differ significantly from mine. There are an infinite number of ways you could divide up the space around the rosettes and you don't have to do it the way I did it. Maybe your lines are set at different angles, or terminate at different points. Maybe they are placed randomly. Maybe they are curved. Don't feel bound to emulate my work exactly, rather, emulate the way I am working. That is the real lesson of this chapter.

MINI MANGLE BOARD 2 (CONTINUED)

To fill the blocked in shapes I follow the existing outlines as best I can, offsetting each new outline about ⅛" from the last.

At this point, if you are filling in the space around your rosettes in a similar style—a field of shapes, each filled with concentric shapes—that means you are about to get a lot of practice carving V-groove lines and offsetting a cut from an existing line by eye. This is good. Even if your first-time results are not as clean and pristine as you would like them to be, this kind of repetitive work will do wonders for you the next time you pick up the knife.

To say that a carver has "good technique," is to say in part that they have committed an awareness of the physics of their tools and materials to muscle memory. To understand immediately what muscle memory feels like, consider what it is like to use a fork and a knife to cut food and get it into your mouth. Consider how little attention you pay to all the precise muscle movements and coordination that action requires, and yet you only rarely make a mistake in the process.

Muscle memory creeps into your actions only through rep-etition. Whether you are aware of it or not, every time you pick up the knife to carve you are

Each shape is filled in with concentric shapes made of V-groove lines.

I follow the existing shapes as best I can, but I'm not too concerned about making the concentric shapes "perfect."

The overall effect is lively to the point of being eye-popping.

The final step is adding a zig-zag border that matches the rosette borders. This repetition helps to unify the board as a whole.

Look closely at the border of this board. It shows the stages of carving the second set of triangular chips. The first and second cuts isolate the chip the final cut along the grain releases the triangular chips.

committing those movements and coordinations to your body's memory. Strive for good technique and good results, and even if your initial results aren't beautiful, trust that you are banking muscle memory that will make every future cut cleaner and more effortless.

For the border I'll return to the zig-zagged triangle pattern I used in the borders of the daisy wheel rosettes. Before I start carving I draw another pair of lines to define the border width —approximately the same as the width of the rosette borders. I leave a little space between the border and the carving, creating a band of uncarved wood that surrounds the carving and joins up with the band of uncarved wood surrounding the rosettes.

I space the inner row of border triangles by eye. You can see that I'm batch cutting them and this batch of first-cuts is also how I determine the spacing, marking them out with the knife. After the first row of triangles is carved, I finish up the border by carving in second row ordering my cuts as pictured.

MINI MANGLE BOARD 3

I chose a wider board (relative to its length) for the final mini mangle board because I wanted to try a leafy vine border similar to some I've seen on folk-carved mangle boards and I knew I'd need a little extra space to either side of the central design. I also wanted to try a semi-freehand grid pattern for the spaces around the rosettes. As for the rosettes, I decided to do one large daisy wheel in the center with smaller "Seed of Life" rosettes flanking it.

I did a lot more layout and design work for this one before I started carving. The board is about 7.7" by 16," but as in the previous two mini mangle boards, these dimensions are somewhat arbitrary. The layout was determined first by estimating how much space I needed for the vine borders along the sides. After a little experimentation I marked the width of those bands first, about 1.5" wide, leaving a 4.5"-wide central field for the rest of the design, and drew a centerline along the length of the board.

When blocking out a design like this it typically takes a little experimentation before I am happy with the layout. I sometimes erase and re-draw part or all of the design before I decide it is time to start carving. To make things easier on myself in this regard, and to prevent the board from

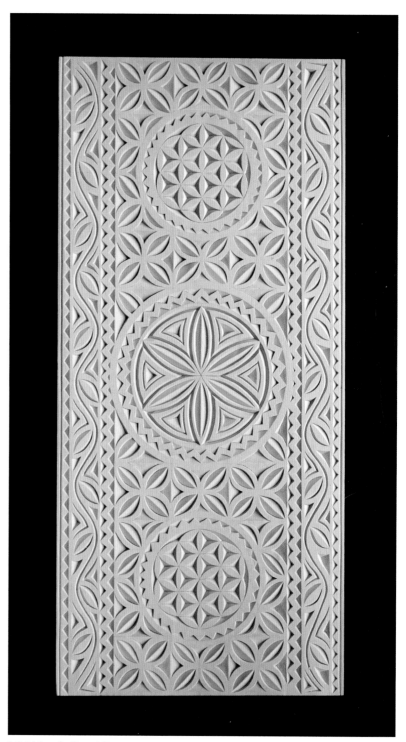

Mini-Mangle Board 3

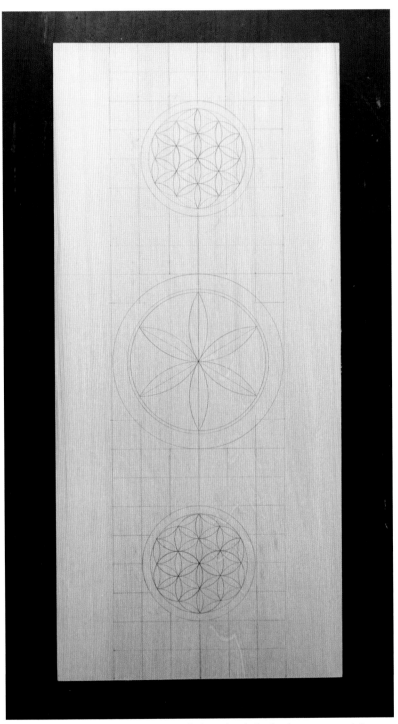

The initial layout of the third mini-mangle board includes both rosettes and the surrounding grid. The details will develop little by little as the piece is carved.

becoming too much of a smeary mess strewn with ghost pencil marks, I draw very lightly. It's easy enough to go back and darken lines if necessary.

I drew the outer circle of the large rosette first, tangent with the lines that marked the borders. Then I used the dividers to break the spaces on either side of the large rosette into a grid of (roughly) ¾" squares. Lastly I laid out the Seed of Life rosettes in the center of each gridded field. As you will see later, I make little tweaks here and there to the layout as I go to make everything work together.

MINI MANGLE BOARD 3 (CONTINUED)

Carving begins with the large daisy wheel rosette. I'm carving by eye, once again using the lines I've laid out as visual guides. I want the petals to be surrounded by a thick band of uncarved wood, so I offset my cuts about an ⅛" inside the drawn petal shapes. My first two cuts for each petal define the overall shape, and something else very important—one of the stylistic elements I'm going for with this piece is mixing high-angle cuts with low-angle cuts. I make the first two cuts for each petal at a higher-than-standard angle. Then I relieve the chips on either side of the petal's centerline with a lower-than-average angle cut. Check the "Changing Angles" section in the Freehand Carving chapter for a refresher on this technique.

For the chips that run parallel to the grain, I shave down to the centerline gradually, removing them in slivers instead of a single chip. This will help keep the wide facet of the chip pocket clean. If you try to remove the chip as a single piece, you will likely cause the wood to split ahead of the knife, leaving a rough texture. To be frank, I'm okay with that sometimes, but this is a very conspicuous part of the carving.

The petals for the central rosette are carved with a mix of high and low angles. The first cut is a high angle cut, the relief cuts are low angle cuts.

To achieve a lower angle of cut, use a First Position grip but extend your index finger. In some cases cleaner results can be achieved by shaving away the chip in multiple passes instead of trying to remove it all with a single cut.

The fill pattern for the spaces between petals is a wide V-groove outline, the same shape carved with a thinner V-groove line, and a mixed angle triangular chip in the center.

The triangular chips for the border are spaced by eye and carved using a mix of high and low angle cuts. The first two cuts for each chip are made at a high angle with the knife almost perpendicular to the surface of the wood.

The relief cut for both sets of border chips is made at a low angle with the index finger extended.

Next I outline the fan-shaped spaces between the petals with bold carved lines, being careful not to damage any of the delicate little points where the lines intersect through excessive undercutting or thoughtless order-of-cut choices.

Next I fill each fan shape with a concentric outline and a single triangular chip. The triangular chips are carved by making two high-angle cuts from the point to the base, and relieved with low-angle cuts. I want to use a heavy zig-zag pattern for the rosette's border so I begin laying out the inner row of triangles by eye with a pass of high-angle cuts to define one side of each triangle, followed by a second pass for the other side of the triangles. The chips are relieved with a low angle cut and the process is repeated for the outer row of triangles.

MINI MANGLE BOARD 3 (CONTINUED)

After completing the center daisy wheel rosette and its border I carved both Seed of Life rosettes, giving each a simple border of triangular chips. I also added an additional circle around the Seed of Life rosettes to separate them from the background grid pattern.

For the leafy grid pattern I'm using the grid as a visual aid for spacing. As with the daisy wheel petals, the first two cuts for each leaf are made at a high angle and define the overall shape of the leaf. The chips are relieved with low angle cuts. If this pattern is starting to look familiar, that's because it's also in the "Changing Angles" section of the Freehand Carving chapter on page 131.

I fill in the rest of the grid with leaf shapes and use the newly-drawn circle around the rosettes as a boundary line to separate the grid from the rosettes, removing the chips in batches to reduce the number of times I have to turn the board.

Pay special attention to how I removed the chips around the rosette boundary line—even though the line itself will not be carved, conforming the edges of the chips to the boundary line allows the rosette to "sit on top" of the grid.

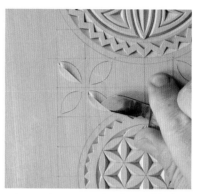

The stylistic theme of mixed high and low angle cuts is continued in the gridded leaf pattern around the rosettes. This helps give the piece a unified look.

The Seed of Life rosettes occupy the center of the grid on either side of the central daisy wheel rosette. Note how the band of uncarved wood around the border intersects with the grid pattern to give the appearance that the rosette is "on top" of the grid.

The diamond-shaped spaces between the leaves of the grid are filled in with three-cornered chips, once again carved with a mix of high and low angles. The curved sides of the chips echo the surrounding leaves and the straight side of each chip conforms to the grid itself.

The next step is to fill the spaces between the petals. These chips are also carved using a combination of high and low angle cuts, conforming the relief cuts to the rosette and border boundaries where necessary.

For the leaves that "emerge" from behind the large daisy wheel rosette I make two additional cuts along the boundary, then remove the chips on either side of it, again using a combination of high and low angle cuts and conforming the shape of the chips to the boundary lines.

Grid chips that intersect with the rosette borders are carved to conform to the borders, contributing to the appearance of the rosettes sitting on top of the grid.

MINI MANGLE BOARD 3 (CONTINUED)

The rosettes and the leaf grid are now complete. I add a zig-zag border on both sides, and new boundary lines about ⅜" from the edges—the same width as the zig-zag border. I use dividers to measure out twelve equal divisions along the new boundary line and square lines across with a combination square. These divisions will act as guides for carving the vine.

Though my vine border was inspired by examples of similar borders and motifs I had seen on a number of carvings, it's not a direct copy, and I spent some time working out a few variations of it on shop scraps before I tried carving the real thing. There were a couple that I liked but didn't fit the carving stylistically, so they didn't make the cut this time but very well may make it into future work.

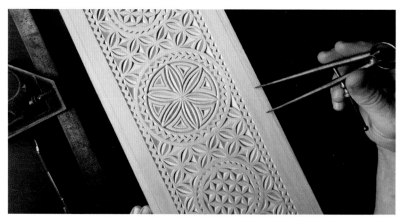

Layout for the border starts with defining a column on each side of the board, then dividing each column into twelve equal segments.

The segments are marked with a combination square. These divisions will be used as visual aides in spacing the leaves of a vine border.

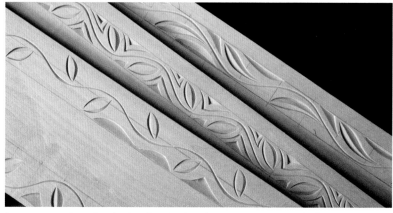

I spent some time developing the vine border pattern on scraps before committing it to my mangle board.

I use the division marks to as guides when carving the wavy V-groove line for the vine border.

Waste-wood from the wavy V-groove is still attached at the points where the curve becomes parallel to the grain because I decreased my depth of cut at these points.

The first step in the vine border is to carve in the vine itself which I do, first, by making one long swooping, full-depth cut along the entire length of the board, using the cross marks as guides to evenly space the curves (more or less.) I'm not going for absolute perfection or consistency from one curve to the other, but rather a smooth, flowing line that stays within the space I've allotted for the pattern. The relief cut can be a little tricky, and requires some very specific and careful knife control. I suggest a few practice runs on scrap before attempting it on your workpiece.

The knife will have a tendency to "run" along the grain at the points where the curve is parallel to the grain. To carve the vines cleanly you have to make sure the knife goes where you want it to, and the way to do that is to *alter the depth of the cut* as the knife approaches and rounds the curves. As your cut approaches the apex of the curve, gradually bring the tip of the knife to about half-depth so that you are only severing the surface fibers.

MINI MANGLE BOARD 3 (CONTINUED)

Keep going, and just after you pass the curve dive back down to a full-depth cut until you approach the next one. You'll find that the chip (or chips—they typically break into multiple pieces where the grain is short) probably does not pop entirely free from the board. That is because at this point only the upper fibers have been cut. Insert your knife back into the cut ahead of the curve and make a gentle second pass around the curve to sever the fibers and fully remove the chip. Make additional passes if needed and clean up any waste left behind.

Now I begin defining the shapes of the leaves with high angle cuts, and then removing two chips from each leaf with cuts made at lower angles. The overall shape of the leaves are the same as the leaves in the grid, but I want these leaves to have a distinct top and bottom, to give a sense of direction, so I carve away a wide-ish low-angle chip along the bottom, and a narrower chip along the top, leaving a little un-carved wood running through the middle of each leaf. This gives them a slightly sculpted look.

Next I fill in the spaces bellow each leaf with v-shaped marks—they look a little like shark fins to me. The negative spaces inside each shark fin-shape and above each leaf are filled in with

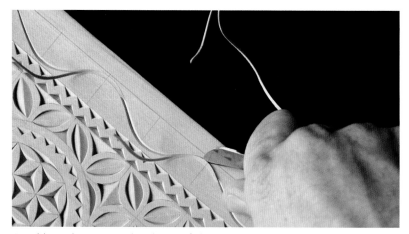

An additional pass around each curve fully separates the waste from the board.

The first two cuts for each leaf define the overall shape. These cuts are made at a high angle.

The relief cuts for each leaf are made at a low angle.

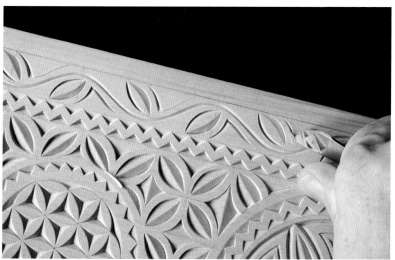

The spaces around the leaves are filled in with fin-shaped marks that echo the shape of each leaf, followed by three corner chips that echo the same shape. The three-cornered chips are carved using mixed angles.

Shaving away waste with multiple passes at a low angle helps achieve a clean facet. This is especially true when the relief cut is made in line with the grain.

three-cornered chips, following the contours of the spaces they fill and made with a combination of high and low angled cuts. To finish this piece I use the remaining space along the edges to add another border of triangular chips and one bold line.

A final note: For all the projects in this chapter I have filled up all the available space on the boards. That is, of course, optional, and you should feel free to experiment with how much or little negative space you work into your designs. I have two reasons for working this way in these projects. First, it is a nod to many of the folk carvings from around the world that inspire me. The tendency to decorate the entirety of a piece's surface— sometimes referred to as horror vacuui, Latin for "fear of empty space"—is a recurring theme in vernacular decorative work of all kinds. My second (and more relevant) reason for covering every inch of these boards with carving is to demonstrate for you a wide variety of patterns, treatments and techniques that you can use to build your own designs.

8 | FINISHING

Finishing wood is an art unto itself. It requires practice, experience, more than a little patience, and, often, a willingness to experiment. Many books have been written on the subject by woodworkers far more qualified to do so than myself (I recommend paying special attention to Bob Flexner's books and blog posts on finishing). My intent with this chapter is not to offer an exhaustive treatment on finishing chip carvings, but to provide a mix of suggestions, observations, and aesthetic opinions. In this chapter you will find a few options for finishing carvings that are relatively easy (if not entirely foolproof), that will enhance the look and feel of your work, and broaden the range of creative effects you can achieve.

SPRAY POLYURETHANE

Spray polyurethane is not very romantic, but it is an good choice for finishing carvings in a number of woods, including basswood, if you want a "natural" look. Multiple thin coats of aerosolized polyurethane will form a thin film on the surface of the wood, which offers protection from dirt, grime, and moisture, while only minimally altering the appearance of the carving. It is also fairly easy to apply and widely available.

Shake the can well before you spray, work in a well ventilated space ,and support your work by placing it on stickers. I use offcuts from the tablesaw ,but an easy substitute is bamboo skewers for grilling or small dowels. Spray it on in overlapping passes with the can about 10-12" from the work.

The key with rattle-can poly is to not go crazy with it—two to three light ,even coats are all you need .Start by aiming off to one side of the piece, depress the nozzle ,and make a steady pass all the way across and completely off the other side of the piece .Not too fast ,and not to slow .If the finish is forming puddles, drips, or curtains, you are moving too slow or are holding the can too close. If the surface color doesn't look at least a little wet ,you're probably going to fast or are too far away.

Several small pieces can be spray-finished simultaneously using continuous, even, overlapping passes with the spray can.

Supporting the work to be sprayed on "stickers" allows even access to the edges of the piece.

Before spraying, shake the can well and test the nozzle for obstructions which may prevent a clean spray stream. Begin spray passes off to one side of the piece, moving at a steady rate across and entirely past the surface you are spraying.

Overlap your spray passes until the entire surface is evenly coated with a light coat. A general rule of thumb for finishing is that several light coats tend to produce better results than a single heavy coat.

Follow the manufacturers directions for dry times between coats and allow plenty of time for the final coat to dry (at least 24 hours) before giving the piece a final, very light sanding to remove texture from the spraying. For sanding, I use a piece of used 320 sandpaper or sanding sponge. Be careful not to sand to hard, especially around edges, so as not to cut through the polyurethane film finish. Be aware that polyurethane will yellow, or "amber," the natural color of the wood a little at first, and that the ambering will intensify a bit over time.

One final suggestion about polyurethane, which applies to finishes for carvings in general: stick to satin gloss polyurethane and avoid the use of semi- or high gloss. This is, I confess, something of a matter of personal taste, however, remember that the visual impact of surface carving is dependent on the play of light and shadow. High gloss finishes tend to "compete" with the work itself, causing every little inconsistency to reflect light and announce itself loudly to the eye. If you are unsure how a finish will affect the final overall look of a carving, do a small test piece first. Time spent testing and experimenting with finishes is never time lost.

PASTE WAX

Paste wax is not a particularly resilient finish, but it is suitable for carvings in light colored woods such as basswood that will not receive much handling, such as small decorative work meant to hang on a wall. The chief benefit of paste wax, in my opinion, is that when it is dry it looks almost as if there is no finish on the wood at all. As with spray polyurethane, it is widely available at hardware and home improvement stores.

To apply paste wax, I use an inexpensive chip brush trimmed with a pair of scissors to make it a little more stiff. Work the wax into the chip pockets and across the surface of the carving, then wipe the brush down with a paper towel or use a fresh brush to go back over the carving and make sure no wax has built up in the chip pockets. Allow the solvent in the wax to evaporate and buff the surface of the carving with a clean lint-free cloth.

The application process for paste wax is rather vigorous, so it may not be suitable for carvings that are extremely delicate—such as carvings with a lot of fine cross-grain ridges between adjacent chips.

Work paste wax gently and sparingly into the carving with a trimmed chip brush. The solvent in the wax will temporarily darken the color of the wood.

Use a clean brush to pick up and spread any wax that accumulates in the chip pockets. Do this as many times as it takes to get a thin, even coat on the surface and facets of the chip pockets without wax built up in the bottom of the pockets.

DANISH OIL

If I'm being completely honest, oil finishes are my least favorite finishes for chip carvings, especially for a light colored wood like basswood, because the oil soaks into the exposed end grain of the chip pockets and creates the effect that the entire carving has been "softened." To my eye, carvings finished with Danish oil always look a little soggy, or spongy. But that's just my opinion, and you know what they say about opinions. If you like the look of Danish-oiled carvings, the good news is that it is probably the easiest finish to apply.

Use a chip brush or rag to apply the oil liberally, let it sit for 10 minutes and wipe off the excess. Let it dry thoroughly before additional coats.

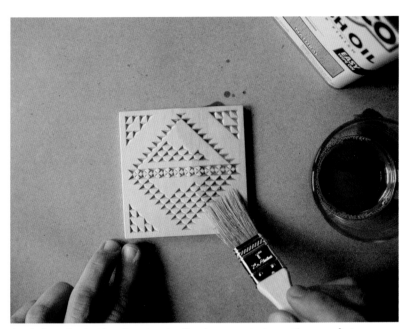

Apply Danish oil with a clean brush, allow it to penetrate per the manufacturer directions and wipe it down well.

The exposed end-grain of basswood is very absorbent and will darken far more than the surface grain.

MILK PAINT

Painted chip carving is not uncommon in the historical record. Many mangle boards of Northern Europe ,for example ,were often carved and then painted bright colors. Color can bring a carving to life by differentiating it's constituent elements from one another and from the whole. In the case of the Minimalist Flower patterns from the First Projects chapter, I used color to emphasize the stylized representation of foliage versus flower.

I am a big fan of milk paint for the same reason that some people seem to dislike: It can be a little unpredictable, so there's always a sense of the final state of a milk-painted object being something that is revealed to you after the fact, not unlike glazes in pottery (though in the case of the flowers, there were no big surprises.) To that point, it is probably a good idea to do some tests with the paint you plan to use for a project, especially if you've never used milk paint before.

There are a couple popular brands of milk paint, both come in powder form and must be mixed with water (this is true for all real milk paint—there are faux milk paints out there that are actually just acrylic paint mixed with a matte medium). I mix my paint to about the consistency of

Milk paint must be mixed with water. A little experimentation before painting a carving is advisable.

Mix the paint well, let it sit for 15-20 minutes to allow the particles of paint powder to fully absorb the water, then mix throughly again. If the paint is thicker than heavy cream, add water in small increments to thin it.

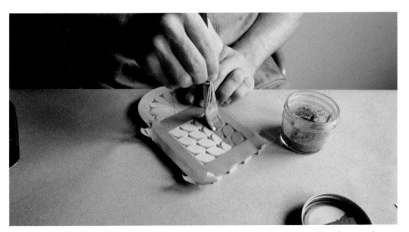

Distribute the paint evenly across the carving, dabbing down into the chip pockets to ensure all the facets are painted.

Use a dry brush to pick up paint that pools in chip pockets and redistribute it across the surface of the carving.

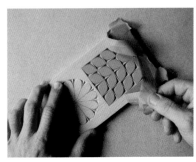

Wait until the paint is dry to the eye and to the touch to remove the masking tape.

Masking irregular shapes requires a little ingenuity. Lots of small pieces of tape can be used to mask curved shapes. Make sure that each piece of tape forms a good adhesive seal with the area of wood it is masking.

half-and-half—this means ignoring the instructions on the packaging and doubling the ratio of water to paint powder. The brand I use calls for a 1:1 ratio, but I use 2 parts water to 1 part powder. Let the paint sit for about 15-20 minutes after it is mixed, and then remix before applying. (When I mix a large quantity of paint, I strain it through a micro-mesh paint strainer.)

After taping off the section I want to color, I use a 1" artists brush to apply the paint. The paint will puddle a little in the chip pockets, so try not to load up the brush too heavily with paint. If it does puddle, you can wipe off your brush on a towel and go back over the puddled chip pockets, using the dry brush to pick up excess paint and redistribute it. It is a good idea to practice this on a small carving before trying to paint a larger one.

It is not uncommon for the first coat of milk paint to look like crap when it dries. Don't worry! Give the dried first coat a *very light* sanding with a piece of used 220 sandpaper, remove all the sanded paint dust, and give it another coat. The second coat will dry and leave an even, matte finish. After the second coat dries, remove the tape.

GEL STAIN

Darker woods with more visually prominent grain, such as butternut, take gel stain exceptionally well. Before staining I apply 2-3 light coats of spray polyurethane as a sealer, to help the wood take the stain evenly. I brush on the gel stain with a trimmed chip brush, making sure to work the stain into all the nooks and crannies of the carving.

Next, wipe the stain off the surface of the carving. I wipe off as much as I can, then use a cleaned brush to pick up stain left in the chip pockets. I repeat this process as many times as it takes to get an even look. My goal is for the wood itself to look darker, not as if it is covered in stain. If the stain isn't wiping off the way you want it to, use a rag and brush very slightly dampened with mineral spirits to help lift the excess stain off the wood. I continue working this way until I'm happy with the appearance.

Carvings in darker woods with prominent grain, like butternut, look good stained because the stain creates contrast between the carved and uncarved areas.

Carvings to be stained should first be sealed to ensure the stain goes on evenly.

Use a clean chip brush to distribute the stain evenly across the surface and facets of the chip pockets.

Clean the brush off with a rag and rework the piece, picking up any areas of concentrated stain and redistributing it as evenly as possible.

Wipe off the excess stain. Keep wiping until you achieve an even appearance.

A little solvent (I use odorless mineral spirits) on a rag helps pick up even more excess stain for a lighter, more evenly stained appearance.

Once completely dry, stained pieces should receive another one or two light coats of polyurethane, followed by a final *extremely light* sanding to remove the texture of the spray poly. Be careful not to sand through the poly and the stain, especially on the ridges of the carving itself and the edges of the board, box or object.

I like to use a piece of old, used fine sand paper, either 320 or 400 grit. For the final sanding, used sanding sponges work well, too, as long as they are very fine in grit and clean. The goal is not to remove any material, but merely to knock of the tiny particles of sprayed polyurethane, the "nibs," and leave the surface smooth to the touch. Follow up by dusting the piece off and wiping it down gently with a clean, lint-free rag.

9 | PATTERNS

The patterns in this chapter correspond to projects
throughout the book, from the practice boards through
the Roman Capitals alphabet. The patterns are printed
here at 100% scale, meaning that they are the same
size as the versions I carve throughout the book. The
ones that are not symmetrical— both practice boards,
Triangle Mountain, and the alphabets —are printed
backwards; all of the patterns can be photocopied,
or scanned and printed on a toner-based printer, and
transferred directly to your workpiece with no need to
resize or reverse them.

PRACTICE BOARD 1

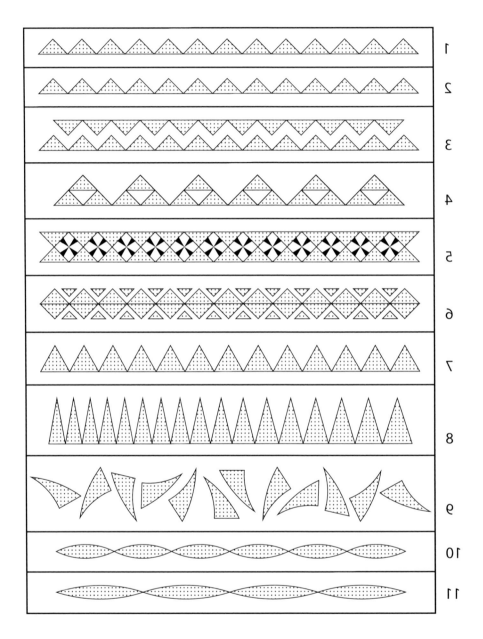

PRACTICE BOARD 2

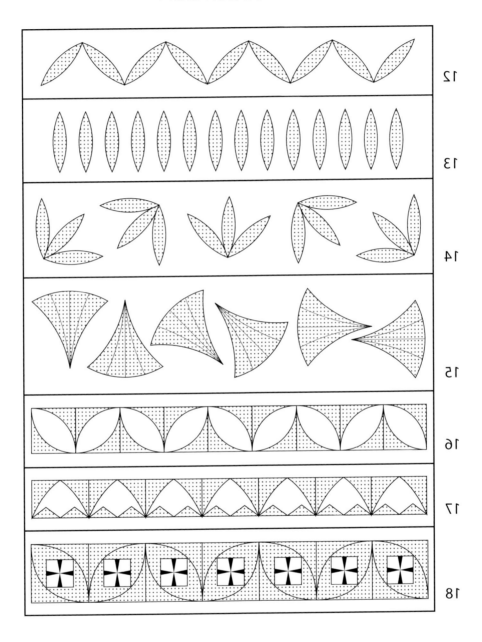

12

13

14

15

16

17

18

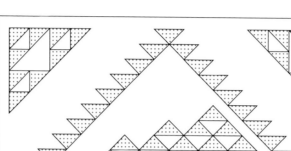

TRIANGLE
MOUNTAIN

SQUARE
ASA-NO-HA

HEXAGONAL ASA-NO-HA

TULIP POT

SEED OF LIFE VARIATIONS

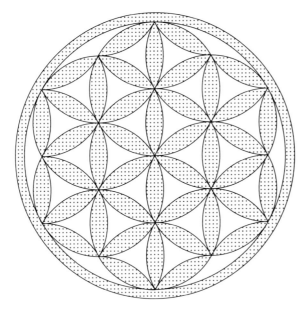

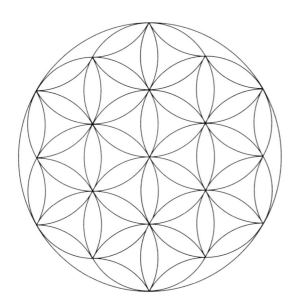

MINIMALIST FLOWER 1

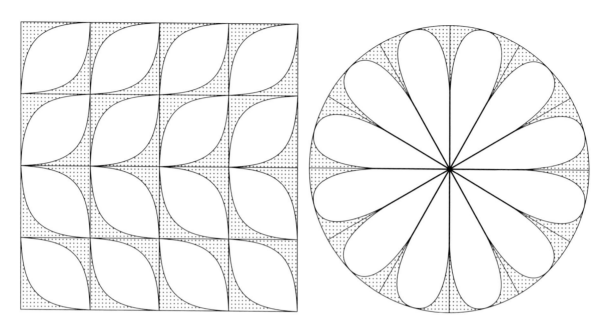

MINIMALIST FLOWER 2

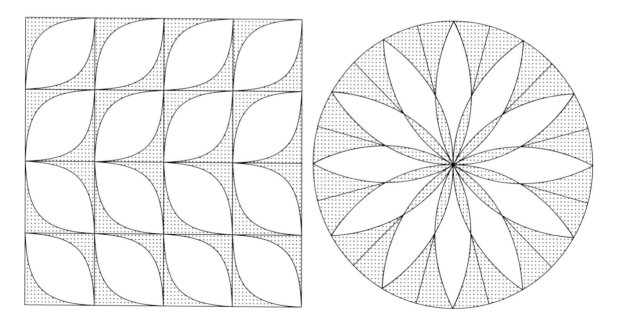

COW'S NOSE

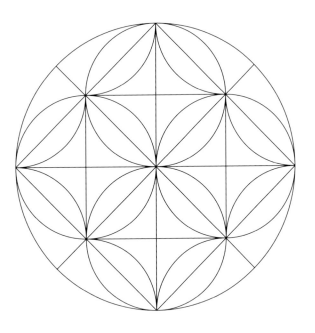

CHARLES HAYWARD BOX

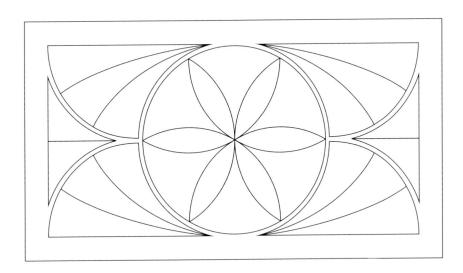

COMPOUND CHIPS PRACTICE BOARD

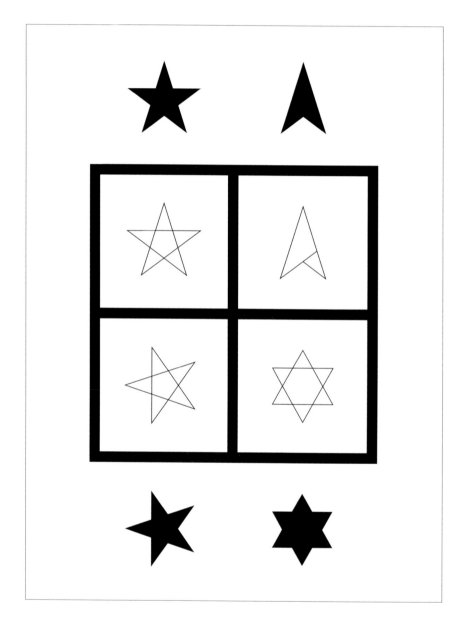

KELLS GRID

ELDER FUTHARK RUNES

ELDER FUTHARK RUNES

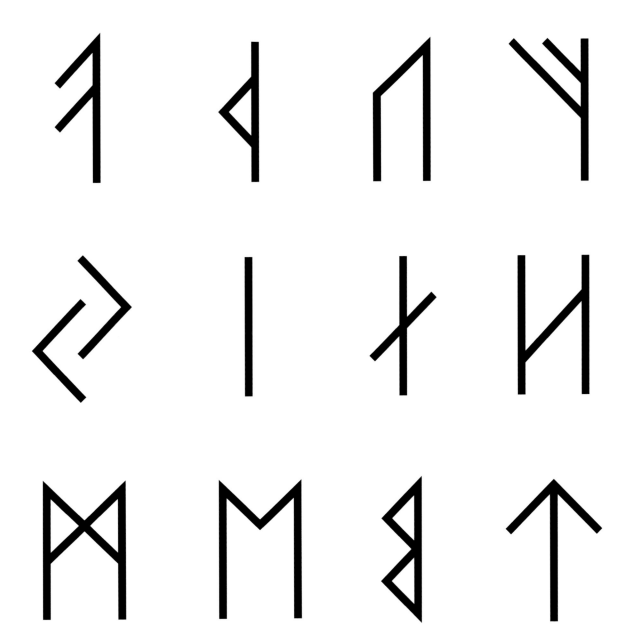

ROMAN CAPITALS

EFGHIJ

OPQRS

XY&Z

67890

ROMAN CAPITALS

ABCD

KLMN

TUVW

12345

INDEX

ABOUT THE AUTHOR

Daniel Clay's route to chip carving was a circuitous one, beginning in 2005 when the desire to take a break from life as a professional musician led him to take a position as an apprentice boat builder at the Carpenter's Boat Shop on the coast of Maine. After stints in timber framing and kitchen cabinetry, followed by a decade in the video production business, he turned his attention to woodworking full time in 2015. Along the way, he taught himself chip carving. Daniel was at first aided by the books of Wayne Barton, and later engaged in a deeper, ongoing personal study of the craft in its various incarnations throughout the ages and around the world. He has written about chip carving for *Fine Woodworking Magazine* and also travels and teaches chip carving at venues around the US. Daniel designs and makes custom furniture, home decor items, and artwork, many of the pieces featuring his carving. In addition to woodworking he enjoys photography and making videos of his work process. You can keep abreast of what he's up to by following his Instagram account @danielclay. Daniel lives and works in Knoxville, Tennessee.

MORE GREAT BOOKS *from* BLUE HILLS PRESS

Projects from the Minimalist Woodworker
$24.95 | 168 Pages

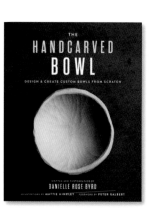

The Handcarved Bowl
$27.95 | 248 Pages

The Art of Kumiko
$24.95 | 168 Pages

Build Better Boxes
$24.95 | 176 Pages

BLUE HILLS
— PRESS —

Look for these Blue Hills Press titles at your favorite bookstore, specialty retailer, or visit *www.bluehillspress.com*.
For more information about Blue Hills Press, email us at *info@bluehillspress.com*.